Praise for *SalesBurst!!*

"Filled with sales stories at once informed and amusing, *SalesBURST!!* is a great read. The planned distribution of profits from the book adds to the warm spirit it engenders."
 —Ken Blanchard, Coauthor, *The One Minute Manager*

"Every salesperson wants to get up to speed as fast as they can—but not as fast as their manager wants them to. *SalesBURST!!* helps every new salesperson shift into fifth gear without skipping first, second, third, or fourth. This makes three people happy: the manager, the salesperson, and the salesperson's banker."
 —Jeffrey Gitomer, Author of *The Little Red Book of Selling*

"This is a great book that shows you how to make more sales, faster and easier than you ever thought possible!"
 —Brian Tracy, Author of *The Psychology of Selling*

"*SalesBURST!!* is an entertaining, clever, and out of the box approach to selling. I recommend reading this book to anyone involved in selling today."
 —Peter Handal, CEO, Dale Carnegie & Associates, Inc.

"Learn from Pat Evans and *SalesBURST!!* how passion, determination, and an intelligence-based sales effort can make you successful."

—John Calamos, CEO, Calamos Investments

"I have utilized Pat Evans' sales methods to successfully manage my sales accounts, my sales team and my career for 17 years. I look forward to using *SalesBURST!!* to train my sales people first hand."

—Joel Leetzow, Board of Directors Member and Executive Vice President North America Scancode

"*SalesBURST!!* is filled with Pat's success stories, which will both inspire you and provide helpful hints to help you meet 'your own quota.'"

—Susan Bulkeley Butler, Author and CEO of the SBB Institute for the Development of Women Leaders and the first woman partner at Accenture

"Pat completely exceeded my expectations. Not only did his presentation provide tremendous insights on sales but it also provided even greater life lessons."

—Rick E. Ridnour, Ph.D., Northern Illinois University Department of Marketing

"*SalesBURST!!* teaches you to set goals and train for those goals so you win."

—Buddy Melges, America's Cup winning skipper and Olympic Gold and Bronze Medalist

"Took your book with me and read the whole thing. I think it's a great read, very entertaining! It was especially interesting to read it this week on the road as I attempted to close the largest deal I've ever done!"

—Matt Perrigo, Vice President of Sales EVCOR

"Reading this book could be the best thing you've done all year. This is a real world story that anyone can identify with. I was hooked with the first chapter. Read this book and you will prosper!"

—Al Lautenslager, Coauthor of *Guerilla Marketing in 30 Days*

"Everyone is a sales person and each of us will be better at it by reading and living *SalesBURST!!*"

—John R. Powers, Emmy Award winning playwright, author and speaker

"If the question is, 'How can I become a successful money maker?' then search no more...Pat Evans has come to show you the way in plain and simple language."

—Tom Dreesen, entertainer and opening act for Frank Sinatra

"I just wanted to say thanks. I have been into a lot of negotiations lately and I think about all I learned from you. You are a great teacher and great leader as well as a mentor. I find myself using lessons I learned from you frequently. It's no wonder EVCOR was so successful."

—Mark Sherony, President, MarXam LLC

The unique SPECIAL OFFER, which can save you $20 is found on the last page of this book!

SalesBURST!!

World's Fastest
(entrepreneurial)
Sales Training

PATRICK EVANS

BICENTENNIAL
1807
WILEY
2007
BICENTENNIAL

John Wiley & Sons, Inc.

Library of Congress Cataloging-in-Publication Data

Evans, Patrick J., 1951-
    SalesBURST!! : world's fastest (entrepreneurial) sales training /
    Patrick J. Evans. p. cm.
    Includes bibliographical references and index.
    ISBN 978-0-470-15071-9 (cloth : alk. paper) 1. Selling. I. Title. II. Title:
SalesBURST!!
    HF5438.25.E92 2007
    658.85--dc22

                                                              2007008124

Josie, my life since 16
Shenade, God's little blessing
Lauren, God's little firecracker
Brettski, "the baby of my baby"

Contents

Contents

Acknowledgments

I want to thank all the EVCORs and all our wonderful customers.

Special thanks to Matt Holt, Executive Editor, John Wiley and Sons, Inc. He's a smart negotiator with a sense of humor who can sure spot talent—me.

I am especially grateful to my dad, Bish, John Calamos, Ken Blanchard, Brian Tracy, Jeffrey Gitomer, Peter Handal, Buddy Melges, John Powers, Tom Dreesen, Harvey Mackay, Susan Bulkeley Butler, Al Lautenslager, Jim Casey, Rick Ridnour, Conor Cunneen, Matt Perrigo, Joel Leetzow, Mark Sherony, Ron Brent, and my niece Bridget Evans.

I'M ON A MISSION to help my niece, Bridget, who has Spina Bifida. I am donating 50% of the net profits from SalesBURST!! to help pay her medical expenses and 5% of the net profits to the Spina Bifida Association of America.

About the Author

Patrick Evans is an acclaimed speaker, sales trainer, positioning specialist, author, and entrepreneur.

He has appeared on *This Morning* (CBS), NBC, ABC, WBEZ, WGN, WYCC, and FOX . Interviewed by the *Wall Street Journal, Newsweek, LA Times* and *Chicago Tribune,* he has been the spokesperson for the nationwide NOMDA network.

Patrick Evans

- Started EVCOR out of his house and sold it for $60 million. EVCOR shipping software/integration facilitated the packages shipped for Intel, Dell, Abbott Labs, Oracle, Ameritech/SBC, Sony, and 3,000 other firms.

- Is a INC. 500 winner with a growth rate of 1,019 percent (ninth fastest growing company in Illinois).

- Helped start up 22 successful businesses.

- Has a Bachelor of Science in biology, minor in chemistry.

ADDITIONAL ACHIEVEMENTS

- Inducted into the University of Illinois—Chicago Entrepreneurship Hall of Fame.

- #1 sales rep nationwide for Singer/Friden within four months of graduating from college.

- Youngest sales manager in the history of the nationwide Singer/Friden Corporation.

- An expert at selling shipping/mailing systems, e-commerce systems, intangible leasing services, and software integration.

- #1 at selling software/integration in North America.

SalesBURST!! represents the fastest entrepreneurial sales training methodology ever created. Entrepreneurs, sales managers, and sales reps all need to learn how to sell FAST.

Preface

EVCOR, which my wife, Josie, and I started out of our house in 1979, was sold at the peak of the Internet Bubble for $60 million. Our firm and its ideas helped 20 people become millionaires. People who know our history have continued to tell me to write a book describing the unique business philosophy that came to be known as *SalesBURST!!*

SalesBURST!! begins by you isolating yourself so you cannot be interrupted. While growing EVCOR, I also helped grow a family with my beautiful Josie. We had two girls and one boy so I have a minor in noise control. Usually I would flee to the upstairs bathroom with a pen and a notepad, close the door, and dwell on one thought. One of the secrets of *SalesBURST!!* is you have to write down one thought and not allow any other thoughts to be viewed on the screen inside your head. OOOMMM... yes, I admit it's already sounding Buddhist but think of it as suburban business Buddhist which will pay off like a slot machine with a metal allergy.

The *SalesBURST!!* thought process allowed EVCOR to increase sales dramatically and enabled me to transcend the typical day-to-day business routine. It begins by acknowledging, in writing, what your best talents are. What are you really good at? If you run a sales force, acknowledge the best attributes of each rep. Achieve your next quarter's sales quota by emphasizing a game plan that is positive. For example, if one of your reps is a terrific closer, pair that rep with one who is a fantastic bird dog for leads. The *SalesBURST!!* methodology also relies on the digitizing of your competition. Once you discover your competitor's true strengths and weaknesses by writing them down, you can then strip away their perceived defenses and design an original attack. Examples of how to outthink a competitor are sprinkled throughout this book.

SalesBURST!! is good at describing how you can take what I call "helicopter shots" of business situations. Simply pick a problem you have, isolate yourself, and allow the 90 percent of your brain, which never sees the light of day, to send a solution directly to you.

Write it down!

You will see this request many times throughout this book.

Write it down!

Sit down with a pad of paper and a pen. Lock the door to whatever room you choose to hide out in. I'll go out on a limb here. I don't know you but I'm convinced if you take a breath, clear your mind and write down a problem you are experiencing, an idea/solution will surface and help you out.

Here is how it works:

Write the problem down in great detail. I AM NOT SELLING ENOUGH is not thorough enough. You must force yourself to crystallize the issues. Write down as much detail as you remember concerning the problem. Once you have been honest with yourself on paper, you will send yourself a series of solutions. Read the entire book and come back to this page and attempt this again. You will be shocked that it is so simple, yet it works every time.

Push the envelope. Push yourself.

Late Show with David Letterman: FAST Close

As I remember it, David Letterman had a guest on his show who was one of the top sales reps in the country.

Letterman: Sell me something.

Sales Rep: How about your pen?

Letterman: Okay.

Sales Rep: How often do you use your pen?

Letterman: Every day.

Sales Rep: Why do you use THAT pen every day?

Letterman: It's my favorite pen.

Sales Rep: Would you pay $2.50 for it?

Letterman: Yes.

Sales Rep: Done.

What is the Object of Entrepreneurial Sales Training?

SalesBURST!! is the fastest process utilized to convert a sales candidate into a producer who can close sales.

I have discussed the difference between "product knowledge" and "closing a sale" with thousands of sales candidates. Do you know which one they choose when I ask which is harder to learn? Yep, "closing the sale."

Every salesperson can, and will, learn product knowledge. The reason they quit or get fired is they can't SELL that knowledge to anyone with a wallet.

I push sales candidates through a very fast sales training course that emphasizes their talents and teaches how to think like an entrepreneur. The first half day I ask them questions about our firm and its products, and if they know (or guess) the answer I continue. The second half of the day the rep travels with a top rep and sees the future.

My wife, Josie, who is very good at taking tests, once told me her two secrets for success: (1) Never change an answer (stick with your first choice) and (2) read one more chapter than the teacher tells you to.

SalesBURST!! will allow entrepreneurs and sales managers to train sales reps to: (1) Sell by relying on their intuition and (2) sell with more confidence since they will be exposed immediately to how an entrepreneur actually sells.

If you want your sales force to think outside the box, you had better treat them like there is no box from day one.

What is the Object of Entrepreneurial Sales Training?

Definitions

Sales. You have a product or service and you want to barter with a prospect that needs or wants it. You get MONEY and they receive the means to cut costs or grow their firm more profitably (isn't that it in a nutshell?).

Burst.

To move energetically.

To emerge suddenly.

To increase intensely.

A flurry of activity geared toward making MONEY.

Fast. I think you can learn quickly. You purchased this book so you can be taught how to make more money NOW. The closing techniques and entrepreneurial mind-set presented here are based on FAST:

Function (Your sales role to perform a specified action).

Adaptation (You will exhibit a modification in behavior).

Sales (You will work very hard and be rewarded).

Training (Accentuate your positives and practice them).

The faster you close (without being obnoxious), the better off you will be. Everyone likes me and I close everyone fast. Think of "closing" as "not giving up." A prospect will admire someone who does not give up easily.

Interactive. Input and output are interleaved (just like in a conversation). This is not your normal, traditional monologue, "it doesn't work" sales training. You will give input, role-play, and learn to be more assertive.

You must write goals down for them to appear important to your subconscious. I teach you to program yourself to be successful BUT you must take notes. Why? Notes are your internal system of organization manifesting itself. Salespeople are notoriously disorganized. I teach you to be functionally organized.

Definitions

Part 1
SECRETS

Secret #1: Ask a Question When You Are Lost

If a prospect says YES and becomes a customer you don't need my training, right?

I agree, so let's start with a NO!

> "We have decided not to go with your firm."
>
> "No, no, no, no, no, no, no, ..."

My teaching methods are based on math principles. Once you have been told NO, what is the percentage that you will still win the deal without my training? Zero percent. Why? You were just told you LOST. Want to still win the deal?

Want to increase your odds when you hear the question, "What are the chances of winning this deal?" If you ask your prospect a question with a YES or NO answer, how much have you increased your odds of winning? Fifty percent? Not exactly. You will have a 50/50 shot at achieving an answer from the prospect. This answer will lead to the next question, which in a few minutes will open up the deal again so you can attempt to win. So the first "secret of closing" is to ask a question whenever you hear a negative (clue: NO is a negative).

I refer to this part of the training as The Crossroads. When you reach a crossroads and you are lost ... ask a question.

The real secret is to run your entire sales career based on simple math principles. Every time you have to make a decision, simply apply a percentage to the consequences. I'm talking about basic common sense math. You don't need a calculator for this.

Are prospects more apt to believe you HAVE TO CLOSE a deal at the end of a month? Yes, so use that knowledge you have of people to your advantage. Construct a close and call the prospect. The odds are in your favor when the prospect believes you are offering a terrific deal. Attempt to close the deal by utilizing "Buy before the end of the month." It works.

Write it down!

What are the odds? Try cold calling, tele-cold calling, e-mailing, blogging, and so on. Apply a percentage to each of the above and concentrate your efforts on the highest percentage actions.

Contact CEOs, CFOs, UFOs (whatever), and also contact the users of your product or service. Apply a percentage to who responds best to your pitch and keep calling on them at other firms. Now you are ready for secret #2.

CHAPTER 2

Secret #2: Prime the Pump

Let's Begin by Starting at the End

I want you to:

- Stand up.
- Look into a mirror.
- Retain eye contact.
- Smile.
- Shake the (imaginary) customers's hand heartily.
- Say, "Thanks for the order! I really appreciate it!"

Now you have experienced the reward at the end of a close. You've WON.

Most entrepreneurs and sales reps receive commission/ payment after a deal is delivered (which could be months after a close). The thrill is in the close.

The role play above, "Thanks for the order! I appreciate it." will be your new morning exercise program. Perform it each A.M. so you start your day with a close. No one else teaches this. Try it. Program yourself. It works.

If you want water from a well, you prime the pump. If you want more sales, prime the closing pump. If you do not close a deal once per day, you will become hesitant at attempting to do so. This exercise keeps closing second nature. You will exude confidence and your prospects will notice the difference.

Write it
down!

Prime the Pump!

Secret #3: Role-Play the 10 Perfect Closing Questions

My son Brett, who was a senior in high school, had a lawn maintenance/landscaping business, which was five years strong.

One night he asked me how to attract new customers since I continually talk to my children about how great sales, marketing, and capitalism are.

Immediately I started to ask him questions because I had always taught my kids and my sales forces the only defense a sales rep has is asking questions. I'll prove it to you.

At EVCOR, the shipping integration firm I started out of my house, the sales reps were instructed to ask questions even during their gestation period. All reps were trained in "question-to-question" combat. We informed them to think in the form of questions during the interview process. We even instructed them to not answer a direct question from anyone when they left our building the first night of training. Please remember EVCOR achieved Inc. 500 status. That means we grew 1,019 percent over a five-year period. Believe me I've hired a ton of sales people.

When I interviewed potential new saleswomen and salesmen I always presented them with my high energy, Who Is EVCOR? pitch. At the end of the questions and answers, which lasted one hour for a first time interview, I asked the prospective rep to sell me something simple like a pen. We would role-play a close. Let's try it.

You and I will now experience the pressure of this type of interview. When I instruct you to give me an answer you promise (hold your right hand up) not to read any further until you commit and answer out loud. My off-the-cuff comments will be displayed between brackets [ ].

Pat: If I was hiring you to type and be a receptionist I would present you with a typing test to ascertain speed and accuracy, right?

Interviewee: Yes.

Pat: Okay. Since you say you can sell, I want you to sell me something. Do you have a pen with you?

Interviewee: Yes, I do.

Pat: Can I see it?

[If it is a beautiful and expensive pen I pull a bland BIC pen from my pocket. If the pen is cheap looking I pull an expensive pen out.]

Pat: Great, now here are the rules. I want you to sell me this expensive looking pen. Let's pretend I purchase pens in gross lots (144) and have 20 left. I will give you a break and allow both pens to sell for the same amount. You have to sell me. Okay? GO!

[INSTRUCTIONS TO READER: DOG-EAR THIS PAGE. CLOSE THE BOOK. PLACE A MIRROR IN FRONT OF YOU AND SELL INTO THE MIRROR. ANSWER OUT LOUD BEFORE YOU READ MY INSTRUCTION!! You must verbalize your answer before you continue to read or you will not learn. Sell me the expensive pen. Go!]

[PLEASE OPEN THE BOOK AND READ WHAT OCCURS IN A REAL-LIFE INTERVIEW.]

[9.5 out of 10 reps take the nervous road and lose all eye contact while proceeding to look directly down at the pens lying next to each other on the conference room table.]

Interviewee: Okay (pause), this more expensive pen (reaches out and picks expensive pen up) is better looking, and you being an executive, it will blend with your professional surroundings. This pen is better because it does not have a cap, which can fall off and be lost. This pen will last longer because it offers a replaceable ink cartridge.

[When the interviewee exhausts every imaginable feature and benefit statement he or she sheepishly queries me.] "Would you like to buy these pens?"

Pat: No.

Interviewee: Why? [The interviewee is now very flustered. He or she has run out of features to comment on and can taste the pressure.]

Pat: I don't need them. I already have pens. [I never explain why the sales process was truncated. I simply place myself on the spot and start to sell.]

Pat: Okay, let's switch and I'll sell you the pens. I'll follow the same rules and your job is NOT to buy from me. Remember, don't buy from me.

Pat: Hi. my name is Pat Evans. What is your name? [I ask while shaking the interviewee's hand.]

Interviewee: Bill Johnson.

Pat: Bill, this is the pen you use now, correct? [Gesturing toward the BIC pen.]

Interviewee: Yes.

Pat: What do you like about the pen?

Interviewee: It is dependable.

Pat: Great. What do you not like about it?

Interviewee: I tend to lose the cap.

Pat: Fine. Which of the two pens looks more professional?

Interviewee: The one you are selling.

Pat: Okay. Please allow me to summarize. This pen [I point toward the pen I am selling] is more professional looking and has a retractable point which cannot be lost, therefore it will last longer. Do you agree?

Interviewee: Yes. [Of course he or she agrees. I ascertained that a few sentences earlier.]

Pat: [I lean to my left and pull a plain white piece of paper from my briefcase. I write PURCHASE AGREEMENT in large letters at the top and begin to fill in the name of the interviewee under PURCHASER. Dead silence ensues for 30 seconds and then a voice is heard.]

Interviewee: What are you doing? [Looks perturbed.]

[LOOK AWAY FROM THE BOOK. WHAT WOULD BE YOUR RESPONSE?]

[Okay, NOW PLEASE CONTINUE TO READ MY INSTRUCTIONS.]

Pat: [Never ever say, "I am writing up a purchase agreement for you to sign." Do you know why? Because if the potential pen customer is a type A personality he or she may blow up at you. I'm talkin' ballistic. This is why sales reps are afraid to ask for the order. Here is what I recommend saying.

I'm simply writing down what we have talked about and I am going to leave it with you." [Do not say, "Okay?" I look down and continue to write for 10 seconds more. I then look up. Interviewee/Prospect now seems more relaxed. My question to YOU (the reader and/or the interviewee) is who is in control at this point? Yes, I agree. Me. Is the type A personality mad at me? No. I must be in sales heaven. Most reps are afraid to go for the close. They believe it is a timing issue and they may be too early. They do not want to be yelled at. I have been closing sales fast for over 31 years and I still do not know when the best time is so I attempt to close very, very early and often. I now flip the paper around and present it to the interviewee.]

Pat: Is this everything we discussed?

Interviewee: [Scans the document.] Yes.

Pat: Well, if you will please sign the order I would love to have you as a customer.

Interviewee: I do not want to sign.

Pat: [I reach over and slowly pull the paper back so it now sits in front of me.] If your firm was proceeding to acquire the pens, would your name appear on this purchase order or would some person above you have to authorize the purchase? [This question allows an "out" for the interviewee/prospect. He simply states someone else must sign and believes this answer will disconnect the sales process.]

Interviewee: I would need to get another person to sign.

Pat: When would you receive confirmation concerning approval?

Interviewee: One week.

Pat: [I write on the purchase agreement THIS ORDER IS NULL AND VOID IF BILL CANCELS IT WITHIN 10 DAYS. I then slide the document back in front of the Interviewee/Prospect. This close is called a contingency close. Please note one of the largest dollar investments a typical citizen will make is a house. The housing industry is huge and contingency selling is a standard way to close a deal in the housing industry. EVCOR allowed this type of close.] Please acknowledge the terms.

Interviewee: I do not want to sign.

Pat: That is perfectly fine. [I then pull the purchase agreement back into my possession.] You have said the replacement pens are more professional looking and will last longer. I am offering the better pens at a discount so you pay only the reduced price, which is the same cost as your present BIC pens. I am not asking you to order the pens from me. I'm requesting your acknowledgment of the terms so I can hold the price for 10 days. [I slide the document back.] Could you please initial and date the document so I can hold the price?

Pat: [The interviewee usually starts to laugh because they now believe they would sign. To not sign now seems out of character. He signs and I have another fervent convert.]

I then ask the interviewee if they believe I could teach them how to sell. They always say, "Oh, yeah." Remember there are many permutations these questions can take. Always listen, ask a question, and so on—it always works.

As you can see, the best and only true offense a salesperson has is questions. I ask questions early and often. I never presume. I simply ask questions. I always ask two or more questions but once I receive two positive answers concerning the product, I close the deal. Most sales reps sign a new customer by getting a signature on paper or an acknowledgment over the Internet. The faster you can pull a purchase agreement out or start conversing about money issues, the faster the conversation will lead to a close.

Please remember this method has worked for me in selling mail machines, leasing (an intangible), computerized scales, integrated shipping systems to host mainframes and mid-range systems, e-commerce, and so on.

My son Brett listened to my questions and we discussed the theory of SalesBURST!! I explained to him that I always strive to make the product I am selling free. If I gave you $10 and asked you for two fives you would not hesitate to transact the deal. If I can prove that you are spending more money without my product than when you have it I will sell a boatload of products.

I told Brett I would do what I always do next. I would research the subject. I found an article in the *Wall Street Journal* (no kidding) that blared IF A PERSON BRINGS HOME $44,000 PER YEAR OR MORE THEN THEY SHOULD PAY SOMEONE ELSE TO CUT THEIR LAWN.

The article, which I showed to Brett, utilized time-value formulae. Entitled "How Much Is Your Time Worth?" the story would make a great handout to Brett's prospects. What home owner will admit to pulling in less than $44,000 annually? Nada, no one.

So using the techniques found in SalesBURST!! Brett could explain to future customers why they were actually saving money by outsourcing their lawn maintenance. The *Wall Street Journal* (WSJ) represents a valued and trusted advisor concerning financial matters. Brett could still describe his company's unique benefits, but the sale would progress much easier since the WSJ was literally backing his sale agenda.

We finished discussing the potential sales approach and acted out a role-play consisting of door-to-door questions and answers. His firm could now attack the market and theoretically grow faster since a trusted third party (WSJ) was positioned as an expert reference.

You may think this approach is aggressive, yet to achieve any sale you must follow these steps. You agree the longer a close takes, the more things can go wrong. Another competitor could discover the potential deal while cold calling for example.

When is the appropriate time to close? Don't worry about having perfect timing or being a psychic. Start talking about price as soon as you can. You will know faster if your prospect has the funds allocated and whether they think your retail price is fair.

Managers who have reviewed EVCOR thought high-tech sales had to be long and drawn out. Consultative selling was the correct way, they said. Most of us had a minimum of 10 years in the shipping software integration business but we had cut our teeth in the knock-on-doors mailing/shipping arena. You will find out that once a prospect realizes you know what is best for them, they like to talk price as soon as possible. Close faster. Do it.

SalesBURST!! and lawn maintenance are a cut above.

Close as soon as possible.

Review

Name?

Now use?

What do you like?

Dislike?

Which looks more?

Do you agree? Summarize [Slide purchase agreement].

I'm writing ... and leaving this document with you.

Is this everything? [Slide purchase agreement].

Please sign. [Slide purchase agreement].

Person above you authorizes? Approval confirmation?

Write null and void. [Slide purchase agreement].

Acknowledge terms. Fine. [Slide purchase agreement].

You have said. Reduced pricing. So I can hold price.

[Slide Purchase Agreement.] Close.

Secret #4: Call Back the Same Day

Would you buy from someone who didn't call you back? Of course not.

I have a science background (bio/chem) so I always attempt to quantify. We've agreed that NOT CALLING BACK is bad for sales. How long will you wait before you officially designate a DID NOT CALL BACK situation as an I WILL NEVER DO BUSINESS WITH THAT FIRM conclusion?

AAHHH ... "herein lies the rub," as Hamlet once articulated. The longer it takes a sales rep to call you back, the less chance she has of closing a sale.

Want to know a great secret to closing a sale? Call everyone back the same day!

"That's impossible," I hear you yell. "I could never eat lunch or dinner and fit that many calls in during an eight-hour day."

You want to win sales deals, right? This is a perfect secret weapon to achieve just that. All competing sales people TELL prospects that they will work hard, be an advocate for the client, they will respond fast ... blah, blah.

Same day callback is a very easy and inexpensive method for sales reps to differentiate themselves from their competition during the crucial first impression time frame.

All you need to do to look organized, trustworthy, and responsible is call the prospect back THE SAME DAY.

Don't try to tell me you are too busy. I used to start my day by logging on and viewing over 100 e-mails, which I had to respond to. If I could follow the CALL BACK THE SAME DAY advice, so can you.

Let's say it is past 5 P.M. and you have six calls you can't return because you have run out of time. Simply call each of the prospects and leave a short voice mail. For example: "Hi, this is Pat Evans, with evanSales, and I'm returning your call from today. Sorry I missed you. I'll call back tomorrow at 9 A.M."

Why not just wait until the next morning to make the call?

- Read this chapter again. You don't get it.
- What if you get busy the next morning? It sure seems sales reps get too busy to call prospects back because I've been a prospect and I've had to chase sales reps. Plus, if you call the next morning the advantage I am telling you about fades away.

My office was in Chicago so I could keep calling to the West coast until 7 P.M. CST. Most of my return calls to the Chicago area could then be completed between 7 and 7:30 P.M.

The voice mail messages I left never failed to help me stand out from my competitor.

The prospect would notice:

- I called back the same day.
- I was a hard worker (heck, I left the message at 7 P.M.).
- I sounded organized because I planned a return call at 9 A.M.
- I proved to be efficient and reliable since I called at 9 A.M.

I hear salespeople moan that people buy only on price. Not true. Prospects want to buy from organized, efficient people who work hard and follow up on time.

You now know a wonderful secret. USE IT!

Call back and leave a voice mail message after 5 P.M. This is a terrific example of how to change lemons into lemonade. Start using voice mail to your advantage.

Secret #5: Intercept

Have you ever heard the saying, "10% of life is thrown at you and 90% of life is how you react?" Life is based on reacting. If life is mostly reacting, why are you attempting to sell by taking action? Why not let life and sales flow to you?

Secret #5 is learning how to intercept or counterpunch. Have you heard of Bruce Lee, the famous Chinese martial arts hero? Did you know he was on *TIME* magazine's 100 Most Important People of the Century list? Why? Bruce Lee studied all the different martial arts available to him and decided they were too slow. He concentrated on speed. Bruce thought efficiency could overcome tradition. He changed the entire world's view of physical defense.

If attacked he countered his opponent's aggressive actions scientifically. For example if someone tried to throw a punch Bruce figured his opponent's leg was closer to him than the opponent's fist was to his face. Bruce would simply wait for the action and then react by kicking the opponent's planted shin. He was faster and therefore always won with his counterattacks.

Bruce taught his students to "be water" and to flow. His beliefs were based on relieving stress. Why not sell without feeling stress? Want to know how to achieve success without involving stress?

Have you ever been told to be a better listener? You should begin a sale by asking a question about the present process utilized by the prospect. Then LISTEN and make notes.

Every action you take from then on will be determined by what the prospect says, NOT by what you want to say. The prospect will describe the present process. All you need to do is LISTEN, make notes, and ask questions.

> "You mentioned … what do you like about …?"
>
> "You described … what do you dislike about …?"
>
> "Your present system … have you ever …?"

If you react and learn how to counterpunch or intercept, you will change your approach, and your sales negotiations will flow more easily. You will not stress about the next question to ask but will instead take your cue from the prospect.

> Listen … breathe … relax … ask your question.
>
> Listen … breathe … relax … ask your question.

This method of selling will work for large complex sales exceeding $100,000 (warehouse management systems) as well as for small sales of $1,000 (mail machine bases).

If you are feeling more stress than the prospect, you are following a slow, traditional sales process that is outdated and not based on science. Allow interception to tell you when to ask and what to ask.

Listen.

Intercept an issue.

Ask a question.

Listen, and so on.

Secret #6: Land Where You Planned

Some of the most interesting people I have ever met have been sales managers. They are expected to grow their firms and they always find a way to do it. I find they are interested in achieving sales goals as fast as possible.

Ask a sales manager what the definition of *sales success* is and you receive a short, concise sound bite, "Land where you planned."

It's so simple. I love it. What is your plan?

How about sales success in 7 questions?

1. *Market Profile* (Who are you selling to?).

2. *Producer Profile* (Are you aligned with your audience?).

3. *Access* (Do you have admission?).

4. *Affinity* (Do you have previous knowledge of the market?).

5. *Viability* (Is the market big enough to allow you to thrive?).

6. *Appropriate Activity* (What are the pertinent levels of action?).

7. *Accountability* (Are you capable of direct responsibility and answerability?).

Entrepreneurs and sales reps will both be better off if they follow these 7 steps. My favorite is Producer Profile. Are you aligned with your audience? What does this mean? Well, a huge insurance firm performed a study that discovered sales reps who had purchased life insurance for themselves sold more life insurance.

It's called mind-set.

Write it down!

Enthusiasm is caught, not taught. YOU have to bring excitement and passion to the bargaining table. You must be functionally organized enough to formulate a written plan and then you have to Land Where You Planned.

Secret #7: Water, No Ice

Listening skills are really important in sales, right? Here is your homework assignment. The next time you and some friends visit a restaurant, I want you to order, "Water, no ice." Watch what happens. The odds are the person waiting on you will bring a glass of ice water. Why? The same reason YOU don't listen to your prospects. Your repetitive presumptions have formed habits that take time to change.

Speaking of restaurants and listening skills, I once witnessed a waiter who refused to take notes when we ordered our food. I asked him why and he said he memorized each line item. Well The Great Karnack delivered our food and three of the five orders were wrong.

Write down what you want to remember. Learn how to write without looking at the paper like I did while walking briskly though warehouses with CEOs. I made notes of every nuance, and months later I could review my notes and contact the prospect. They were always amazed at my retention level.

They would always ask if I been in there lately. I would always respond, "I listened to you and I took extensive notes. I'm a pretty quick study." If you sell any type of system, I would also suggest you draw a picture of their present layout.

When you practice this, please review your notes the same night. Why? You will forget what some of the notations mean if you don't review them the same day. Trust me, I know.

Write it down!

Listen, Converse, Listen, Suggest Solutions, Listen.

Listen (Think body language and nuance).

Converse (Ask questions that have "time sensitive" answers).

Listen (Write down quick notes, retain eye contact).

Suggest Solutions (Choose one surefire feature your system has that will positively benefit the prospect, and mention it in a question format).

Listen.

CHAPTER
8

Secret #8: The Blame Game

The only way sales reps will become top selling reps or entrepreneurs is if they become accountable for their actions.

I asked different sales managers, "What does a sales training book HAVE TO address?" The answer was universal, "Activity and Accountability."

Let's deal with accountability. Never blame a prospect or a customer. You must blame yourself.

What is *blame*? The dictionary describes it as "responsibility, answerability, accountability, or fault; to be the cause or source of something; to hold responsible." *Fault* is described as "a minor character weakness." This means it is easy to fix (it's minor).

When I researched answerability or responsibility they both were defined as BLAME. WOW. If you could quit blaming others what is the immediate reward? How about *honor* and *glory* because these two words are the antonyms of the word *blame*? Your new path is to accept responsibility.

Blame can be split into two categories: guilt or shame. You suffer guilt when you cause an action. Shame occurs when you begin to believe you are a bad person because of some action you took. Shame has nothing to do with attaining sales quotas and is a destructive force. Guilt can be controlled by taking charge of your life. Act responsibly and you will be perceived as a responsible person. You will then evolve into a responsible rep or entrepreneur and accept blame.

Write it down!

The secret is to ACT responsibly. Tell yourself each morning and after every meal that you are a responsible, take-charge person. You pay for meals with a credit card (it is easier to track your expenses) so place a Post-it note with the word RESPONSIBLE printed on it in your wallet where you store your credit cards. Keep it as a reminder, and let's start boosting your sales.

Secret #9: Give and Take

We all know there are two types of people: those who say, "My glass is half empty," and those who say, "Isn't that my glass?" I'm an "Isn't that my glass?" person. I have learned over the years that negative thinking is a waste of time.

Blaming people is a bad habit that takes up a large part of a typical person's day. I'll prove it. Your homework assignment will be very simple: DON'T BLAME ANYONE FOR ANYTHING FOR THREE DAYS. This includes slow and/or moronic car drivers, your spouse or significant other, your children, prospects, and watch out for this one—people in your own firm. If you mentally blame any person for anything, start over with a fresh three days. E-mail me when you have successfully completed the task, but keep in mind my life expectancy.

When you sell, you always have to be thinking, What's in it for me? This is how closers think. You don't turn this mechanism on and off. You simply think that you may have a better solution than what you are faced with.

I have many examples of this type of thinking but one of my favorites occurred while I was at a party a few years ago at a house in central Illinois. Six of the partygoers had congregated in the kitchen with me. A friend was telling a story and it started to drag. I felt my blood coagulating so I jumped up and yelled, "Hey, what's in it for me?" The guy looked up, noticed everyone's attention was wandering, and fashioned a finale really quickly.

Another example includes a hobby of mine. I have raced sailboats since I was eight years old. My present sailboat has a roller furling jib and mains'l. The outhaul unfurls the sail while a sheet or reef line furls it and vice versa. So every time I utilize a sail by unfurling it, one sheet retracts and one line elongates.

This is how you should visualize a close. If a prospect wants your firm to give a discount or throw in extras, answer yes, but first explain what you mean. For example, a prospect wants money off on a maintenance contract. Okay, but explain there are two types of contracts that you offer. Full price gives the prospect onsite response within four hours. The discounted contract offers a slower response so a technician will show up by the end of the next day. This means the firm's mail or packages will not be sent or shipped out for one or two days. I never once had anyone choose the slow response discounted plan.

Write it down!

Isn't that my glass? Every time you think to blame someone, turn it into a positive. Create a Franklin "T" inside your head and when a negative idea surfaces like the dread you may feel about possibly losing a deal, simply look on the positive side of the "T" and read off the counterbalance, I will succeed and win the deal. Will yourself to think in a positive format. You do not gain any advantage by thinking negatively.

If you feel someone messed up you should create a constructive series of questions to pose to the individual. "When can we expect _____ to occur in your department?" EVCOR once had a manager's meeting and I asked each manager for his and her forecast. You could tell that each manager was experiencing a bottleneck with the administrative team. So I asked the office manager about it and she was not forthcoming with any viable explanations. I stood up and walked over to the whiteboard and drew a picture of a huge parking meter type device and labeled the far left side TODAY and the far right ETERNITY. I then asked the office manager while pointing to the board, "When will the service department have their response from your department?" We all burst into laughter and she promised an answer within one day.

Your SalesBURST!! thoughts affect the entire company.

Secret #10: Be a Contrarian

My wife's father, whose nickname was Bish, was a tremendous sales rep. He started his agriculture business back in 1933. This was during the Great Depression when U.S. unemployment was a staggering 25 percent.

He used to tell me sales stories when I was a teenager (I met Josie when I was sixteen). There was one story I really loved. Bish was selling during the Depression and President Franklin D. Roosevelt had declared a bank holiday for the entire State of Michigan. This means all the banks in Michigan were closed. Most sales reps were driving out of the state figuring no businesses would have money so why try to sell. Bish thought it was an incredible opportunity because his business-common-sense instincts told him all the businesses would be holding money they could not deposit into any bank. He immediately loaded his station wagon to the brim with agricultural products and sped off in the direction of the sale promise land. He was so right. Every business owner wanted to get rid of the money so no one could steal it from them.

They purchased months' worth of product to deplete the excess bucks. Bish sold every bit of product and I am sure he was laughing while he dined on his beloved rotisserie chicken.

I stopped by his home on my way back from attempting to sell my first account. Bish was very happy to see me and wanted to know how my sales career was progressing. I was excited and told him I had just demonstrated a mail machine to a gentleman who was the top purchasing authority at a firm called The Copernicus Institute.

Copernicus was the correct name to bring into this house because he was Polish and so was Bish. After a few weeks of dating Josie I had memorized some of the kids' Polish nicknames: Josephica, Franush, Marishka, and so on. Copernicus was the scientist who had proselytized the theory that the Earth traveled around the sun versus the Catholic Church who stated the Earth was the center of the universe. It's a good thing he didn't know about Pluto.

I sat on the edge of my seat and asked Bish if I could turn the TV sound down so he could hear about my new sale. He said Okay and I turned the sound way down. I started to explain to Bish what led up to my first deal. I had been in sales for only a few weeks and just knew this was a deal. Bish queried me: "Tell me about the deal." I decided to explain every detail. "Well, the man stated I reminded him of his son. He agreed the product would save his firm money each month and thought the price was fine." Bish asked, "How did you close him?" I responded, "Well, he likes me, the product, the price, and so on." Bish sat up straight, "How did you close him?" "I haven't closed him yet but …" Bish sat back abruptly and demanded I turn the sound back up on the TV. I started to explain the deal again and he simply said, "Turn the sound up!"

It's been 33 years since this discussion took place and it is still fresh in my mind. You may think Bish was a jerk for ignoring me but that was his way of communicating to me his disgust. He was a very successful and professional businessman. He certainly knew the difference between being close and closing the sale. At first, I was mad at him but months later, after finding out how hard it was to convince people to trade their money for a product's benefits, I realized it had been a wonderful lesson. If I wanted to be part of this grand fraternity/sorority called sales I had better become a closer. The old saying is correct, "You can't be almost pregnant."

I believe Bish, who passed away years ago, would be very proud of what I have achieved in my sales career. I bet he is in heaven smiling down at me right now with the sound turned up on Channel 5. Thanks, Bish.

My first piece of advice is to follow the rules your firm lays down. If you can exceed quota then continue to follow these rules. If you cannot sell enough to beat your quota, my recommendation is to think like a contrarian. Think outside the box.

Generally accepted sales myths like "Don't cold call during lunch" are flat out not true. Lunchtime is when the receptionist is eating lunch and the boss is more easily accessible. Walk into a firm and keep walking until you meet someone. The person you meet might be the top person.

Always attempt to sell the way your mentor teaches. If you do not achieve quota within 90 days I strongly suggest you examine your approach and attempt a slightly different technique. Sixty days later you must change 180 degrees and attempt a radically different sales approach if quota remains elusive.

Write down your present game plan. What is the title of the person you contact? What is unique about your product, system, or service? What is the compelling part of your offer? Now, examine your answers and change the criteria. Call on a person higher up in the food chain, which means you may have to go over someone's head. *Hint:* Never tell a prospect you are calling a different manager. Simply take the action. Have your product/system/service benefits typed out and compared to your competition. Don't address the fact that another manager in the company does not want to go with your offer. Please remember that once you have been told, "NO" that buyer has made a decision. You only need to change that decision to win the deal. If you can't change the "NO" to a "YES" then locate a different manager at the top of the firm and start selling again. That is a lot easier than finding another prospect, prequalifying, and closing.

Secret #11: Bet on Yourself

How many people here play poker? This is one of the questions I ask my audiences when I speak to sales reps. Hands shoot up all over the place. I've never seen so many people publicly admit to a vice—gambling. I bet you it's an epidemic.

Since many sales reps will bet on cards it should be simple to have them move that confidence level over into quota busting sales.

It's tough to close sales when you play not to lose instead of playing to win. The difference between these two approaches was quite evident when Michael Jordan would demand the ball so he could swish the last shot in a close basketball game. He once noted that he never once thought of missing the final shot. He repeatedly visualized taking and draining the game winning basket.

How about a baseball metaphor? It's very tough on your groin muscles when you keep your left foot on first base and try to steal second. If you can't steal bases it's probably because you think in terms of covering 90 feet faster than the catcher can throw you out. Successful base stealers say it takes only 12 strides to reach second base. They have analyzed the math and know the pitcher gets the ball over the plate in 1.25 seconds. Catchers can erupt and throw the ball to second base in 2 seconds. A fast runner can make it to second in 3.28 seconds after a leadoff of 10 feet or 3 strides. The runner must be perfect and try to get a jump on the pitcher. That is the secret.

Sales reps whose main goal is not to upset anyone at the firm they are trying to sell are doing themselves a disservice. You can't close deals if your game plan is, Don't make anybody mad! Just like stealing second base, you must be focused on one thing: Go for the close, steal the base.

My advice is for the 99 percent of salespeople who are like-able, honest, and offer a fair deal for a fair price: If you are the type of aggressor who is void of personality, makes people mad outside of sales, or lies then I'm not the type of mentor you want.

My methods work for reps who like to interact with people and have a sense of humor. Use metaphors and stories to sell your ideas. I remember when I sold against a specific competitor and a prospect informed me she had decided to go with the competition. She had made up her mind before allowing me to demo my firm's solution.

I asked if she had any daughters or nieces. She was startled and said she had two daughters (I had taken a chance). "Are they married?" I queried and she responded that one was married and the twenty-two-year old was not.

"Let's imagine it is the wedding day of the twenty-two-year old," I said. "Your family has already committed to pay for the wedding and reception, and the wedding couple is at the altar. All of a sudden one of your relatives, who is a detective, comes up to you and declares he knows the groom and the man is wanted for tax evasion. What action do you take as a parent? (1) Allow the wedding to proceed? (2) Pause the wedding and talk to the groom and detective in a side room?"

Every man or woman I have related this story to has selected (2) Pause the wedding. That is when I explain, "I simply need a quick 15 minutes to explain my product and its benefits. I know it is less expensive and is more efficient for your firm. Once you see me you will have reviewed all your choices. Can I see you this afternoon? I'll be there at 2:30."

The secret of the story is changing a business mind-set and allowing the purchasing person to feel the repercussions of a bad decision (personally) in less than a few minutes.

If you are willing to work hard and focus on my strategies (metaphors/stories), you will increase your sales. Many people can't tell jokes but I find a lot of sales types who love to tell a story. Start telling more SHORT stories.

Write it down!

Bet on Yourself! Presume you will win each sale.

Aristotle Onassis, the Greek billionaire, walked a reporter over to a huge window overlooking a Greek seaport filled with his oil supertankers. Onassis proclaimed, "This is what I gamble on." Shift your gambling habit from cards or casinos, where the house holds the odds, to yourself and your sales career where YOU control the odds.

Secret #12: Is Sales Art or Science?

Do you believe a sale is art or science? Let's discuss one option. If you picked science then the principle of parsimony that defines science—the simplest explanation is the best answer—should be acceptable to you.

KISS—Keep It Simple, Stupid is the modern, modified version of that scientific explanation. People appreciate simple explanations. They are attracted to simple solutions. If people feel like they understand, they will buy.

My teaching methodology is quite simple. When you attempt to sell someone they want to know the product's core benefit, the price, and when they need to take action to acquire it. Please note that price is within the first two line items listed in this buying proposal.

I teach sales reps to talk about the price within a short period of time. They are trained to take action. Quote the price but not the full purchase price. If you are selling a house you should quote a monthly mortgage amount and then break it down further into a daily cost. Always break the purchase price down until it is perceived as a minuscule amount, then compare that daily amount to the list of perceived advantages your product or system entails.

Managers in different parts of a company think of labor costs in different ways. You should be aware of this prior to quoting any pricing. For example a manager in the warehouse thinks of the white collar administrative staff as salaried per yearly types. Dock workers and other warehouse labor are thought of in terms of per hourly.

You should start discussing your product's cost in monthly terms and then take it to a per hourly figure as fast as you can. This allows you to set the tone for how purchase price will be perceived during the balance of the negotiation. This is a very important hurdle. If you receive pushback on the daily pricing, please ask the prospect how they usually address costs associated with what you are selling. For example you can ask, "What is your cost if you stay with your present product?" I love this question. Most sales reps never ask it. The prospect will then respond with the real reason you are both sitting there. "Well, our present system is paid for BUT our supplier cannot furnish us with …" BINGO, now you only need to compare your daily price to your competitor's daily price and offer some form of guaranteed service period that is longer than the present supplier's. The guarantee will identify you as a more progressive partner than your competitor, who already appears wounded in the eyes of the customer who is being forced to upgrade.

Write it down!

A sale is based on science. If you agree you can quantify and win; you can compare and win. You can write down the actions taken and determine a different approach. If you agree that a sale is based on science, then you can start to win every deal by making incremental adjustments to your approach.

We have tons of scientific data concerning psychology, emotions, and so on. I agree that you must ask questions (scientific approach) and be recognized as a friendly, trusting personality type (science has already identified the different types of personalities). It seems that most sales reps when properly motivated can sell. Try a scientific approach and your sales will definitely increase.

Secret #13: Immediate Action After Strategy

Immediate action after strategy is what I teach. Do I believe in formulating a profitable strategy? Yes, I do and I find most sales reps and entrepreneurs will study and plan but not take the necessary actions to ensure success after their strategy is in place.

Strategy is *your plan* while Tactics represent *your actions* to achieve that plan. I believe in fast actions to achieve your plan. Write it down and take the necessary actions immediately to achieve the plan. The faster you win or find out your plan was flawed, the faster you can create the next plan and therefore the next swift action. Do not start out of the gate with multiple plans.

Here's a great example I found online. "The number of 'moves' in a tic-tac-toe game is 4 to 5, while the actual number of 'strategies' is over 6 trillion." I don't know about you but I win at T-T-T and I only know about a trillion of the strategies. NOT!

Lack of action is usually why sales reps don't succeed and this directly affects entrepreneurs. I have observed and have read that most sales reps fail to ask for the order. You might ask, "How can a salesperson forget to ask a prospect for an order?" The answer is quite simple. They don't forget; they simply wait for the right time and there is no such thing as the perfect time to ask for an order. Their strategy is to ask but they never take the action.

It's like jump roping with two people swirling the ropes. When is the best time to jump in? No matter what strategy you pick you better move really fast when you take the action.

When EVCOR was a few years old I used to start my monthly (all employees in attendance) meetings by asking:

Pat (loudly): What are we going to do today?

Employees (loudly): We are going to make mistakes!

Pat (loudly): What are we not going to do today?

Employees (loudly): We are not going to make the same mistake twice!

The entire company would move forward the next month very fast and very loose. The employees would take action without being worried about getting yelled at. I can count the number of sales reps on one hand who repeatedly made the same mistake twice. I fired them. All my other sales reps worked hard, repeatedly asked for the order, and won almost all of their deals.

Most sales are not won on originality. The prospect is usually interviewing two or more sales reps before a decision is made. If you continually ask for the order, the prospect (who does not sell for a living) starts to presume you must hear the word YES a lot. Why? The prospect is not in sales and cannot fathom asking someone to buy from them that many times. It's just how people think. They want a supplier who won't stop trying to help them and you are proving you won't stop in your attempt to help them. You become a positive bill-board for what they are looking for.

Write it down!

Football coaches are famous for planning and having a unique strategy. My favorite was Bill Walsh of the San Francisco 49ers. Rumor had it that Bill would script the first 25 plays and his team would run those plays no matter what the outcome. He would then adjust based on what formations the competition threw at him. I believe that you, acting in your sales capacity, will make an appointment, be pleasant, perform a demo and NOT ASK FOR AN ORDER. I believe that the typical sales rep will follow the traditional 25 or so scripted steps toward a sale but never attempt to score. They will attempt to adjust to what the prospect throws at them, but they will simply not score by asking for the order. I say you should at least attempt to close the deal three times. Take the action and go for the win. Ask for the order.

Secret #14: Program Your Mind

Can a better memory increase your sales? Yes, and it can change your life for the better. I will describe the short course of how and why concerning memory retention.

Are you feeling happy right now? Maybe not, so allow me to demonstrate how to program yourself. Please take a sheet of paper and print your first name. Next to it please print the word HAPPY. Write #1 above the word HAPPY and finish by drawing a big smile under the words. Now visualize the entire picture in the color blue.

Close your eyes and envision the entire image. Great! Now I dare you to try to forget it. Go ahead—get it out of your head. You can't. Why? The best way to memorize is to utilize mnemonics or memory tools. If you want to remember important goal-based information, the very best method is mnemonics.

Our minds have evolved over the centuries by interpreting color stimuli through our senses. I always say, "If you want to remember something write it down." Writing a list of items is perfect for grocery shopping. You won't forget anything on your list. Goal attainment is unlike shopping. It is different from looking down and checking off BROCCOLI from a list with no pressure involved.

If you want to attain a goal you must begin by visualizing that goal. Program yourself by viewing a color image. You will remember the image and it will pull you toward your goal.

I never miss quota. I've been in sales for 31 years and every-one who knows me will admit, "He's never missed his quota." People who experience problems such as missing quota each month want to succeed. They tell themselves to succeed but are not programming themselves correctly.

Start using the image method and your sales will increase because the success image will appear over and over again, which will reinforce your actions.

Let's program you to hit quota. Print your first name on the paper; draw an arrow pointing toward the top of the page and then print EXCEEDS QUOTA. My image would look like this PAT ↑ EXCEEDS QUOTA. Now visualize it in the color green. Go. If it helps you remember, place the word EXCEEDS on top of the word QUOTA and/or swoop an arrow under all the words and let it fly up at an angle. If you don't have colored pens buy some.

To consistently beat an ever increasing sales quota you have to remain focused and on task for a month at a time. We all want to succeed. Some people are blessed with more will-power and focus. The image memory method levels the play-ing field and enhances the goal-striving mechanism.

Write it
down!

Visualize the goal, remember the goal, exceed the goal. Print out 10 of these images and place them around your home, your desk, and in your car. You have never tried this so you will be startled by the positive results. Sales is a mental game—get control of your mind.

Part II
QUESTIONING

Answer a Direct Question with a Question

A laugh is the shortest distance between two people.

Victor Borge (comedian/pianist)

How would you like to learn to sell faster? The #1 salesperson in the world can close more deals faster than anyone else.

Let's start. First lesson: Answer a direct question with a direct question. EVCOR sold $40 million per year of shipping software and integration services. Our sales reps were taught to close their deals as fast as possible. At the end of the first day of sales training I would give the new reps their homework assignment. ANSWER A DIRECT QUESTION WITH A QUESTION.

For example when the rep arrived home that night and their friend or loved one asked, "Is that you, Tom?" he could respond, "I'm home. How was your day?"

When I explain this to you it sounds awkward but it works flawlessly in real life. People will answer your question and then you are free to ask a question or answer their original question now that you have more knowledge. Go ahead and smile. Successful attorneys use this method all the time.

Whenever I interviewed on college campuses, seeking to hire new sales reps, I utilized this question principle. I always requested that a minimum of 25 students be in attendance when I presented EVCOR's offer. Group interviewing is very efficient and dynamic.

Pat: [Asking one of the students] What's your name?

First Student: Lisa Edwards.

Pat: Wrong. [Asking the next student] What's your name?

Next Student: Tom Johnson.

Pat: Wrong!

The third student always figured it out and would answer, "Why do you ask?" or "What's your name?" Everybody would laugh. We would then proceed to role play utilizing this technique. Everyone loved role-playing their parts and answering with questions.

You were programmed since you were a little kid to obey authority and answer questions. In sales you are expected to think before you respond. What was the voice intonation? Why is the prospect asking me that question? Is the purchasing agent asking a question that sure sounds like it's coming from the competition? Example: I sold against the largest company in the mailing/shipping systems business in the United States. They had thousands of employees and most of the customers. Prospects would ask me, "How many service technicians do you have?" If my business was only a few months old and I had only two techs I could blurt out, "Two" but I think that sounds small. So I would ask a question, "If you call my competitor for service at 1 P.M. when do they arrive onsite?" The prospect would answer, "Tomorrow." I then asked, "If we guaranteed in writing same day four-hour response time, wouldn't that be better for your firm since you would then get your mail and packages out?" The prospect would always say yes and I would close the sale. Not once in all the years I sold did a prospect then revert to the original question and need to know how many service techs we offered.

If you will role-play this dialogue your sales will close faster. Questions are a sales rep's best offense and defense.

Question: "What are you going to do tonight?" [Write your answer down but make it a question.]

How about: "What are you doing tonight?" You simply took this question and turned it into a question from you. Great and no one will even notice, but you will receive an answer before you have to give an answer.

Here's another one.

Question: Why is your company better than the firm I now have?

Your response? _____

How about: What do you like about the firm you have now?

After the answer ask, "What do you dislike?" This works wonders.

You will find out more info than you hand out. Practice it. Role-play or you will never change your present habit of answering with a direct answer.

Try it.

The Checklist Close

If I have made myself clear, I have misspoken.
Alan Greenspan, Chairman of the Board of Governors of
the Federal Reserve

The number one best closer in the shipping and execution
software business utilizes a checklist closing technique.

A prospect will always expect a discount when the deal begins
to formulize. If the proposition was presented properly, the
sales rep should have accumulated a list of requirements. The
salesperson should gather this information by asking questions and noting the answers of the prospect.

The sales rep should formulate a relationship with the executive involved with the acquisition. You don't have to take
them golfing after the first meeting, but you should have
some personal information that you gleaned from your meeting. An example would be his or her favorite college football or basketball team (depending on the season). Where
was he/she raised? The person's assistant can give you the
birthday, and so on.

Now you are ready to ask questions, as you fully understand the present business model. Once you know the flow of the business you can begin to suggest possible solutions. Years ago, I conversed with four executives of a vacuum cleaning firm. They assembled the units in their local plant. I asked for a tour and we walked the entire facility. When I viewed the conveyor line, I noticed that an employee would place a part, which was already in a cardboard box, into a plastic tote and would push it down the line. The person at the end was forced to unload the cardboard and part from the tote. I asked why they needed the tote. "We have always used the tote," was one executive's reply. When I revisited the plant two weeks later, the totes were gone and I sold a shipping solution. One of the execs told me they went with my shipping solution because they respected my intelligence and instincts.

Following the checklist techniques, you should present your solution and have confidence it will really save the firm money or time. Ask for the order and be prepared with questions if the prospect does not buy.

Let's review:

Pat: I examined your firm's processes and discovered X,Y, and Z. Do you still utilize those processes?

Pat: I then gave your team an in-depth demonstration of our solution. Did your team like the solution? Will it solve the problem I discovered?

Pat: The price of the solution is $___/month and you now spend $___/month for your present system. Do you agree my system will save you money? Then why can't you sign today?

Prospect: THE PRICE IS TOO HIGH.

Pat: What do you believe is a fair price?

Prospect: Your price is 15 percent too high.

Pat: I can offer you a longer-term lease, which will lower your monthly cost and hedge against inflation for a longer period. How about $___per month for 60 months? [The idea is to talk about price. Ask questions about price. Is the prospect mad about the overall price of ownership like maintenance or is it a specific issue with the purchase price?]

Prospect: We will not be leasing. Just lower our purchase price.

Pat: If I can call my manager and we can adjust the cost to $_____ [attempt 3 percent less] will you sign the order today? [Never offer a lower price without first obtaining a guarantee of a signed deal IF your manager can accommodate the request.]

Another checklist point could be maintenance. You can offer a lower purchase price IF the prospect agrees to a multiyear maintenance agreement and supply contract. You make the same (if not more) revenue and close deals much faster. You may believe your net profit will suffer, yet EVCOR had an EBITDA (earnings before interest, taxes, depreciation, and amortization) of 23 percent, which is very healthy. Every customer I ever tried this on closed.

Write it down!

Laydowns are very rare. Automobile dealerships have coined a term for people who walk in and buy cars at sticker price with no haggling over price. These customers are known as "laydowns" and are a rarity approaching extinction. The Internet has slain the laydown since now everyone it seems has access to pricing information on every subject and they all expect a discount off sticker price.

You expect some form of discount at the tail end of a negotiation so why wouldn't one of your prospects? They will, so you should prepare for a discussion concerning price.

If you are the type of sales rep who cannot stop offering discounts, you might try what I suggested to a rep years ago. We bumped his retail price up by adding extras a customer may need like supplies and a maintenance contract included. He could then strip these prices off the page, as the customer wanted a lower price and the rep ended up closer to retail because it lengthened the negotiation process.

SalesBURST!! is manageable.

Land Mines

Err on the side of caution.

An anonymous purchasing manager

A land mine is a bomb, which is activated by stepping on it. You can uncover verbal land mines by asking pointed questions of your prospect. What does my competition say about us? How do you compare our service and response time?

You can plant land mines against your competitor by explaining to the prospect the truth as it relates to the competitor's company. What is the truth? Is the competition promising a certain onsite service response time? If yes, then explain what reality is. Tell the prospect the names of any companies that use the competition and don't like their service.

Do you have any references who now use your system or service that used to be customers of the competition? Call them and ask why they dropped the competitor.

Every company has a weakness: The largest firms with commanding market share can charge higher prices. Attack their pricing. Large corporations sometimes lose control and cannot meet the service response times promised by their sales force. Attack their slow service response time.

Small firms are usually underfunded. Growth eats up cash. Attack their size and potential for nonexistence, which will place doubt in a prospect's mind.

When you personally purchase a product, do you ever really know if the sales rep is misleading you? Don't you ever ask questions like, "How long have you been in business?" Have you ever purchased something and found out too late that what was represented was not what was delivered?

I'm not telling you to make stuff up like some politicians do, but you should expose any lies or misconceptions a competitor may plant in your prospect's mind. You will not know the land mines are there if you don't ask questions.

I once had a prospect tell me he was not going to purchase from us EVER. I said, "Why?" He sarcastically responded that he did not trust our sales rep and would never do business with us again. I was stunned and brought up the name of his present sales rep, and he said that he trusted her but he did not like so-and-so. I asked if I could call him back in 15 minutes. I then asked around and found out that the bad rep who the prospect did not trust now worked (believe it or not) at my competitor's. I called back, told the prospect, and we got the deal.

Write it
down!

The idea is to plant doubt in the mind of the prospect. Never lie. If you lie you are planting a land mine against yourself that when discovered will blow you out of the deal. You do not need to mislead the prospect. Just educate the prospect concerning the competition's weaknesses.

Cats, Dogs, or Fish?

Father: This idea sounds half-baked.

Son: Oh, no. It's completely baked.

Dustin Hoffman (son) in *The Graduate*

Why do sales reps ask questions that don't work and lead to failure? I'll relate a story about my all-time favorite BAD question. It is ubiquitous and, believe it or not, most sales reps in retail sales are taught to ask it.

Many years ago I walked into a pet store in a suburb of Chicago with two of my three children. My kids were ten and five years old at the time. As we walked in, the sales rep behind the counter looked up and said, "Can I help you?" I have always explained any secrets of selling to my kids so I stopped, bent down, and whispered, "Did you kids see what just happened? This guy has been taken over by aliens. I'm going to answer, 'NO, we are just looking.' The sales rep will say, 'Okay' and do something else."

So I did it and the sales rep said it. "I told you!" I said to the kids all excited. Both of my kids' eyes got real big and one said,

"Wow, Dad. You are controlling this guy." I then suggested we help him. "Why don't we teach this rep how to sell? Come on."

We walked over to the counter and I said, "Hey, do you want to make a lot more money? I train sales reps and your technique is all wrong." The sales rep agreed to follow my advice and I told him what to say to be able to sell better and faster. I have absolutely no experience in selling pet supplies and know nothing about the product knowledge necessary to do so, but I am an expert at sales technique and closing people.

"I know you can't make any money by asking, 'Can I help you?' and everybody answering, 'No, I'm just looking.' So, here is the new game plan. When the next prospect walks through the door I want you to say, 'CATS, DOGS, or FISH?' Oohh here comes someone." The kids and I scrambled behind the large 80-pound bags of dog food and turned to listen to the sales rep.

A woman walked into the store and the rep said, "CATS, DOGS, or FISH?" He then abruptly turned toward me and did not hear the lady say, "Dogs." I stood up, sauntered over, and politely suggested he walk the woman over to the dog section of the store. Once the three of us were standing near the correct section I advised him to say, "Dog food, leashes, bowls, or toys?" The lady was smiling from ear to ear and when he said the line she responded, "Dog food." I then suggested, "80 pounds or 40 pounds?" She answered, "40 pounds" and also suggested her favorite brand. He carried the brand and consummated the sale while giving the personal attention he aspired to.

The final part of this sales lesson would have occurred if I had stayed in the store. I would have attempted to sell up.

This method teaches you to sell one more item to each customer to increase sales. I would have said, "Would you be interested in a wider dog collar that would have your home phone number displayed in large numerals so anyone could see it from a distance and call you if your dog was ever lost?"

VOILA! If you work in retail please remember this detail.

Write it down!

Never ask, "Can I help you?" Why? You will receive a response that neutralizes you with no benefit. Your prospect has basically said, Don't bother me. Never ask a question that if answered a certain way may neutralize you.

If you work in retail clothing you can ask, "Shirts, pants, or shoes?" If the prospect says, "Belts" that is great. Walk with them to where the belts are located. This approach can also be utilized to determine which point of the sales process you are in. Ask the prospect, "What do you like best about our firm: our fast service, our product's benefits, the helpful sales rep?"

Alternative Ways to Cold Call

Nothing in life is to be feared, it is only to be understood.

Marie Curie

Which employee in your firm answers to the following description? The person sits at a desk at the entrance to a firm. The employee answers the phone, types, has a little bit of an edge, maybe does the mail and is trained to keep salespeople and other foreign invaders OUT.

Yes, you're right; it's the receptionist—the "white blood cell (WBC)". The only person with "Don't let anyone in who does not have an appointment," listed in the job description and the only employee with a "defend the fortress at all cost" mentality.

So, how do you cold call? How do you as a sales rep get by this person? Believe it or not almost all sales reps exit their car and walk in and try to converse with the WBC. How dumb can you be?

I suggest you simply walk in a different door and experience a totally different reception. Walk in through the shipping dock. Most people working the dock presume you are there to speak to a manager. You simply ask the first person you see, "Purchasing? I'm looking for Purchasing" or "I'm looking for the Sales Manager." Make sure you walk briskly and act like you are supposed to be there. I worked trucking docks for four summers to put myself through college. Ninety-nine percent of people unloading trucks don't care who you are and are not as uptight as white-collar workers. This approach works. I used it when selling leasing and mailing/shipping systems. I cold called with saleswomen and salesmen. Once the rep gets over the fact that they can simply enter through a different door, their prospecting becomes much easier.

Haphazard cold calling is not a profitable venture. You must divide your prospects into niches and match any present customers to each niche. Now you are prepared to cold call more efficiently since you can mention a reference when approaching a prospect.

You can also utilize this technique over the phone. Call a prospect and instead of asking for the CFO or the president ask for "Accounts Payable." Why will the receptionist put the call through right away? Because she thinks you are asking for money and you would not be calling if her firm had paid its invoice on time. She is not paid enough money to screen this type of call, so she allows you past the gates. Once you hear, "Accounts Payable" you simply say, "I'm sorry. I wanted the CFO. Can you please transfer me to the CFO? (do not say *him* because the CFO may be a woman.)" If you are passed back to the operator, please hang up without talking and call back at a different time of the day and try it again.

I have never had to do this more than twice. It works.

Write it down!

Ask questions and ask often. The more questions you ask, the more money you will make. Prospects are people just like you. They want to find a trustworthy supplier and to depend on them.

You can actually save their firm time and/or money but so many sales reps lacking in social skills have approached them that roadblocks are knee-jerked into position when any salesperson appears.

Ask your prospect, "If I can prove mathematically that you are wasting money and can supply you with industry references (industry references trump brand name references) will you purchase my product?" If you receive a YES you are very close to a deal. If they reply NO that is okay. Simply ask the prospect, "How can I get your business?"

Selling an Intangible

First I get confused, then I get afraid.

Leasing Manager

Selling an intangible is very similar to selling a tangible item. Most people believe the major difference is that you can demonstrate a tangible item like a mail machine but you cannot demo a financial transaction. I say you can demonstrate both.

I began my sales career cold calling business-to-business in downtown Chicago. I sold or leased mail machines and mechanical scales for Singer/Friden who was the major competitor to one of the world's largest postage meter firms. This firm represented a virtual monopoly in the mailing and shipping industries it presided over. We used to say we were selling in their sandbox. I became the top sales rep in the nation within four months and the youngest sales manager in the firm's history within two years.

Three years later I left Friden and went to work for a local finance firm, a small leasing firm with offices in a northern suburb of Chicago. Years later it would sell to an East Coast finance firm for millions of dollars.

The drive to the firm was a good hour each morning. I remember sitting at a stoplight about two miles away from the office when I started doubting myself. I thought, What the heck am I doing? Presumably the stress of leaving a job where I was a very well-known icon to selling an intangible like leasing from a dead stop was overwhelming to my subconscious. I gathered myself together and literally said to myself, "I can do this so let's go!"

The president of the firm had recruited me and thought I would be brilliant at assisting sales reps of copier companies close more sales utilizing leasing. He was right. I had no finance or leasing experience but the president, who had a degree in mathematics, believed in me.

My first day was a Friday and I reviewed all the technical books in the president's office having to do with high-level finance. I learned how to read the blue book pertaining to the "present value" of money. I picked out two books here and three books there, and I literally had a stack at the end of the day that when I sat down reached from the floor to my knee. I decided I would read and review all the material by Monday morning.

First thing Monday I sat the president down with his vice president and started to ask questions. "In *Fishman & Perrigo* v. *Sherony, LLC* why did the lessor ...?" They both started laughing. I said, "What?" They responded, "You don't need to know any of that legal stuff. You need to know only how to answer questions concerning our lease rates and how to assist the sales reps under your control. Just do what you have been doing successfully for years—close people."

They were both amazed at the volume of information I had soaked up over the first weekend and reminded me to simply rely on my sales and closing skills because after all that is why they had recruited me.

My dad always taught me to outwork everyone else because you could never count on being the smartest or the fastest but you could always control how many hours you worked. When I was in high school on the wrestling team, my teammates and I would run long distances to get our wind and get in shape. My dad would say, "Run until your heart bursts." I ran and ran, I tried and tried, and I'm still trying. It was terrific advice and I kept outworking everyone else. As a matter of fact my future father-in-law always said, "Pat, you are the hardest working Irishman I've ever met." Years later when Josie and I had three children and had settled in a western suburb of Chicago the local football coach revved up his football team by sending them out on the field half deranged by inciting them to "RUN LIKE YOUR HAIR'S ON FIRE!" They won the game.

The president would sell with authority but he had a math degree and had been in the finance business for years. I was looking for some kind of an edge. When I was trained to sell mailing equipment I always worked off a script. These leasing guys just kept saying do this or do that, but there was no written method as to the sales technique. It was long on art and short on science. With my college chemistry background I always sought to create an organized template to work from. So I shut myself in a room and allowed the Sales-BURST!! thought process to send me an answer.

I decided to create a one-page template of questions the copier sales reps could simply hand to an irate CFO (chief financial officer) who was mad that the leasing company made any money at all on the lease transaction.

The template was very easy to fill out. The CFO or finance manager would supply one answer per line. I discovered I may not be classically trained in accounting at the Harvard Business School but I certainly had a master's degree in people reading skills.

I always wore a beeper, and the sales reps from the different copier companies would beep me if a CFO did not like the leasing amount or had questions concerning anything to do with the lease. When I began I had zero sales reps. Within six months I had thousands relying on me to help them close deals. You see, I sold each copier firm's sales manager by promising to help increase sales AND manage the sales force. My competitors offered only lower lease rates. I positioned myself as a sales manager who would cost them nada. How have you positioned yourself in your territory? I would help the copier companies increase the total amount of sales they booked each month by acting as an extension of their management team. The copier company in essence would receive a very talented sales manager and an increase in overall sales, yet keep their lease rates untouched.

The problem the copier sales reps had encountered was CFOs who would always explode when they multiplied the monthly lease amount times the term of the lease. Before I invented the template, that had been the end of the lease deal and the sales rep had been left standing there trying to sell a $20,000 copier with a two- or three-year payback. Not good.

The first question for the CFO on the template was, "Have you remembered to subtract the tax from the total since your firm has to pay the tax whether or not you buy or lease?" Most of the time they had not subtracted the tax, which the sales rep had included since it was the law. BINGO. I was on the phone with the CFO for less than two minutes and already had achieved a modicum of trust. The CFO was not yelling about the total any more and was willing to listen.

The second question dealt with the firm's rate of return concerning the dollars invested in their business. "Do you receive a 13% return on dollars invested in your business?" This was a loaded question since no CFO wanted to tell someone they had just met on the phone that their firm did not receive a certain return on investment, so they would always say "Yes." Bingo! Now I could insert this number into math formulas.

For example leasing offers a hedge against inflation. Simply insert the present rate of inflation (%) and presume it will remain the same for the term of the lease. If inflation is low at the moment then allow it to increase each year in your model.

My job was to calm the CFO and explain the true benefits of using someone else's money (leasing). Instead of NOT purchasing a money saving device because of its upfront cost, simply figure the monthly cost and compare it to the monthly savings. If the savings outweigh the cost, utilize leasing.

In summary, if you sell an intangible remember you are still requesting a prospect to trust you AND give you money based on their belief that money spent with you will always be less than the solution being paid for. How does this sound? I want you to give me $40,000 and I will present you with only $10,000 worth of savings over five years." I bet you never close anyone. Ever.

83

Questioning

If you sell an intangible, create a template. Allow the prospect to fill it out and then sit down and walk the prospect through the questions. If this procedure is performed correctly you will have a convinced prospect that will quickly become a convinced customer.

Good Selling. SalesBURST!! is intangible.

Write it down!

Always sell utilizing a template that is simply a list of questions for the prospect. Figure out which question will bug the prospect the most and ask it first (like the tax question in the copier lease scenario). Be prepared to answer that question so your answer helps alleviate the prospect's concern. A template forces you to organize your thoughts and your presentation. It will obviously make you look good since you took the time to compare your firm's products and services to the competition's.

Part III
LISTENING

Self-Monitoring

*I started calling myself a genius to impress people
and ended up being one.*

Salvador Dali

P*sycho* is a pretty strong word. It connotes someone out of control. What happens when you add the word CYBERNETICS to psycho? You achieve psychocybernetics, which by definition is "the fine working of a machine called the mind."

I am a firm believer that my mind controls my body. Just look around the world today and observe the ever increasing level of obesity and you know not everyone shares my opinion.

Psycho Cybernetics is a wonderful book written by a plastic surgeon, Dr. Maxwell Maltz. I consumed this book during my sophomore year in college. It's a short yet powerful book that changed my life. My major was physical therapy before reading the book, and then I switched to biology once I had digested its meaning. It taught me to believe in myself. It strengthened my core belief that Pat Evans was smart and could achieve.

Dr. Maltz refers to many patients who walked in with physical and mental scars. He could drastically change their looks but many never achieved confidence in themselves and acted as if they still had the debilitating physical blemish.

His main theme is that happiness is within the boundaries of your own mind. Train your mind and achieve.

I started to add positive rituals in my life. Whenever I took a shower I would program myself by repeatedly thinking, I am great on the in breath and R-E-L-A-X on the slow exhale. That's 10 minutes of positive reinforcement each day. It worked. Most people perform zero minutes per day of self-confidence building. They instead wallow for hours in self-pity and negativity. Whenever I felt doubt in any form creep into my consciousness, I would breathe more deeply and practice this exercise.

While a biology major in college, I read a paper that hypothesized that self determined positive reinforcement would work just as well as receiving affirmations from others. So, if you want to be successful in a rejection riddled world, you will need to muster positive energy. You can have your mom call you 20 times a day and say, "You are terrific, Honey" (an image of George Costanza's mother enters my mind). Or you can program yourself by utilizing the breathe-great-relax method, as well as by visualizing every aspect of your upcoming sale and imagining positive reactions.

You can achieve any goal that is consistent with your internal mental blueprint or picture of yourself. If you believe the sort of person you are cannot cold call and be successful, then all your sales training is a waste. It's that simple. You have to recognize who you think you are and then discuss with your subconscious who you want to be. Once you have completed these mental sessions with yourself all new training and goal setting can be accepted.

Are you struggling to hit quota? Do you perform the cold calls to hit your monthly goals or do you start a little late, eat a longer lunch, and quit early because the results are not forthcoming?

You have a belief mechanism that acts as your compass. You have added to your beliefs ever since you were a kid. We all tend to remember defeat more vividly than success. Have you ever read a sports story about a famous successful athlete or coach? They can always remember exactly what occurred in a defeat. These same successful coaches and athletes visualize success and program themselves to win. They remember defeat but they dwell on success.

You will not win all your sales deals. The idea is for you to convince yourself now that you have worth and people should purchase from you. If you lose an occasional deal, you will be stunned and won't worry about losing again because you will not allow it to happen.

Write it down!

Do you want to be liked or respected by prospects? Don't dodge the question by claiming you want both. Pick one. If you picked "liked" then you will have a very tough time hitting sales quota. If you selected "respected" you will be viewed by prospects as someone who should be trusted, followed, and respected.

You may be chafing against my advice right now. I can hear you yelling, "Hey, I seek to be liked and respected!" I'm a very likable person. I will tell you all my best sales reps were likable people, and I hire only likable people who exhibit empathy toward others. All wanted to be liked by everyone else and then they met me. I would retrain all new sales reps. The idea was for them to remain likable (which you cannot change) but they had to focus on the attributes within themselves that attract trust and respect through assertive take-charge behavior. Role-play or real life experience are the only ways to build this assertive personality.

How to Calm an Irate Customer

*The truth is that emotion is part of the mechanism of reasoning.
The lack of it is very detrimental to decision-making.*
Antonio Damasio: Professor of Neurology, University of Iowa

How would you react if one of your recently sold and installed customers called you into a meeting at their facility, sat you down, and just started yelling at you?

Well, here is how I recommend you handle the situation. First, allow the person yelling to keep venting for a few minutes. Pull out a pad of paper and take short notes without losing eye contact for long stretches of time. After a few minutes interrupt politely and apologize to the venter by saying, "I apologize for any problem my system may have caused, but if you could please not yell and simply describe in detail what the issues are, I will take extensive notes and attempt to rectify any issues immediately."

This response will work because the yeller wanted to set a tone. You allowed the tone to be set and now you can inject calm into the situation.

At one particular meeting, I listened to an executive who was a successful businessperson: the executive was approximately six-feet tall, and requested that 10 people sit down in the conference room. The exec then jumped right out of the chair and started yelling.

An apology coupled with extensive note taking will diffuse any emotional situation, like the one I described.

After the executive had finished, I asked each of the employees attending the meeting if they could explain the issues each experienced. The exec agreed and the first person started to speak. I stopped the person and asked him his name, and then asked him to continue. I wrote his name next to his explanation, which I feverishly wrote down in shorthand. Shorthand, by the way, is just very fast writing where you are probably the only human who could ever decipher the scribbling.

Once everyone had talked, I asked each of our engineers to comment quickly and then asked if we could tour the system to see for ourselves.

We took the tour and within 15 minutes 2 of the firm's managers were in a disagreement over the first issue. I wrote their names down and noted their comments. Within 30 minutes the visual evidence provided us with a few more facts.

It's tough to install viable software when one manager signs a document describing how the original system operated and a second manager contradicts him after the new system has been installed.

To be fair, the manufacturer of the software had failed in some ways to improve the speed of the system, but the extensive note taking diffused an emotional situation. The notes I had taken in the conference room did not match the reality I found during the system tour.

FACTS: Our firm had very few disgruntled customers and had built a sizable business. I believe the customer is always right and simply desires success. I want every single customer to be happy and pleased with their decision to place trust in me and my firm.

Hopefully this story will help you diffuse a tense situation some-day. As you know EVCOR sold hi-tech shipping software and integration. Selling software is unique from the standpoint of what exactly the deliverable is. EVCOR decided the deliverable should be spelled out in a 53-page configuration document. It featured large typeface and screen prints so the prospect could easily see exactly what they were buying. We also requested the prospect to initial every page in the lower left-hand corner so no one could accuse us of switching pages after signature.

Our sales force had originally fought management on this but ultimately sold it as an advantage because we appeared so organized to our prospects.

Write it down!

Take extensive notes and date every communication you send or receive. I take extensive notes. This is part of becoming functionally organized and it will help you deal with potentially hostile situations. Functionally organized means you have and use a filing system in which nothing gets lost. You don't have to duplicate work.

Take notes and become better at negotiating in a tense atmosphere. Remember to ask pertinent questions while keeping eye contact and break any huge problems into smaller issues to be resolved.

I'm sure you have faced some issues in the past. Now you can discuss them as issues to be rectified.

Part IV

HIRING

The Most Efficient Interview

Most of us present ourselves as who we wish we were. And the conflict between that idea and reality is always fascinating.

Peter Sarsgaard, actor

Need to increase sales volume in your territory or business? Welcome to the hiring dilemma. First, I'll explain the problem with traditional hiring and interviewing methodology with the emphasis on SalesBURST!!

1. Costs you money to place an ad.

2. You need to read each resume.

3. You must call each interesting prospect and play phone tag.

4. You must sell each candidate on attending an interview with your firm (10 to 20 minutes).

5. You must interview each candidate.

6. If the candidate does not show up you still allot the time. This filler time is less beneficial than structured organizational time such as SELLING.

7. If the candidate attends the interview, you lose from 30 to 60 minutes even if you know in the first 3 minutes you will not hire this person. Ever.

Question: What sales manager or entrepreneurial owner of a small business can afford to waste 30 to 60 minutes per interview? No one I know. That's equal to one full day's productivity thrown out the window if you interview only eight candidates. Believe me, there are loads of losers whose resumes look pretty good.

The very first time you experience this waste of time, you will question the waste of production time, but you will attempt the process again because you are still faced with the hiring dilemma. Eventually, and eventually occurs really fast, you will give up and dedicate your precious time toward increasing your own sales, convincing yourself hiring is a waste of time and does not offer tangible productive results.

I have seen the process repeated over and over again by very capable sales managers and business owners. They are not stupid. They understand they need more sales reps but cannot afford to miss sales quotas by partaking in a flawed interviewing process.

Issue: Their territories or businesses will eventually stall out at a certain level because they need more leads/presentations/quotations/closes to grow sales volumes properly.

Solution: Shrink the time necessary to hire new sales representatives.

How to Hire Efficiently

1. Place an ad and have the candidates e-mail their resumes to your firm. Utilize a "signal" name like Bob

or Judy Thompson to send their resumes to. Do not use your name.

2. The resumes will be collected by your receptionist or assistant. Any phone calls can be handled by them. They will realize that a sales candidate is calling because the "tag name" is being deployed. The receptionist/assistant can simply state that sales interviews are being accepted to fill a position. "Please choose either 9 A.M. this Tuesday or 4 P.M. this Thursday," the receptionist/assistant will state without discussing anything about the firm. They can tell the candidate to review your firm's web site and to be on time.

3. When the candidates arrive, have them fill out a new hire sales template form, which you can purchase at any stationery store. Why? It will demonstrate their neatness, if you cannot decipher their writing it might be prudent to take a pass.

4. You only have to be ready at exactly 9:15 A.M. when you have your receptionist/assistant bring you all the resumes. Review them quickly and circle any pertinent information that will remind you of a conversation you can start with each representative.

5. Showtime. Collect the resumes and walk to the area or room where the candidates are waiting. Introduce yourself and explain that you will be conducting the interview. Make sure you have not booked more reps than available chairs in one room. I would usually not invite more than 12 people at one time.

After the candidates have all been seated in the conference room, sit down with them, select a resume, and call out that person's name. Place that resume in front of you and call out the next name. Place this resume to the left or right of the first resume. You will place each resume in the order the candidates are seated so that you can call out a name and know where that candidate is when you begin to ask questions. So, if you want to speak to Jim you would know he is seated to your left and that he is two people away from you. Each resume will have about a half-inch showing so you can see the rep's name and still conserve space, six resumes to your left and six to your right.

I could look around the room and tell instantly who had a chance to be selected based on interviewing 99 percent of the successful reps already with my firm. I'm not talking gender or race. I review grooming, dress code, eye contact, and charisma.

I hand out a single piece of literature on my firm, and ask the reps to peruse it while I quickly view their resumes again.

Now, I start to ask a few questions from the circled high-lighted items on their resumes. After I engage each rep for a few minutes, I select a rep and ask that person to describe EVCOR as if I were a prospect.

The description is usually one-dimensional and not sales oriented. I then describe EVCOR as if I were selling a stock; lots of sizzle and enough terrific facts to entice the prospect to ask questions because they want to know more. My description is found in Chapter 24.

I then have one of the candidates sell me a pen. After they try to sell me and fail, I guarantee I will sell them AND

I instruct them to please not buy from me. This sales process was described in Chapter 3.

Why do I hire this way? I can interview 12 candidates in one hour without any preparation time on my part. All 12 candidates will want to work for me because I taught them how to sell during the first half hour of our meeting. If only 1 candidate out of 12 shows up, I'm not inconvenienced. In one eight-hour day, I could complete interviews with approximately 50 applicants. That is 10 times more than traditional methods.

You can also visit local colleges when they offer "hiring days." I request that 25 students be in attendance for my 30-minute hiring presentation at any college I visited. The college would always agree and I received much more exposure than my competitors.

Good luck with the old, traditional way of hiring sales reps if you need to bulk up your sales force each year. It will be very slow.

Write it down!

Group interviewing is the future. Here is the major problem with the traditional process used in hiring sales representatives. Two months after trying to find the one perfect sales rep and wasting a zillion hours of their personal sales time, sales managers throw their arms up and meet the quota with their own personal sales. Owners of businesses find themselves in this predicament every few years.

This process repeats itself and must seem like Groundhog Day and the manager/owner is Bill Murray. The manager gives up and for 12 months can meet quota. All heck breaks loose the second 12 months when the company misses quota by a wide margin.

Go New. Go Efficient. Go Group.

CHAPTER

24

Rejection and Impression

Friends of mine started a distance running program down in North Carolina. On the back of their T-shirts is a slogan: THE MIND IS THE ATHLETE. So your mind is key.

Bill Rodgers, Olympian and four-time winner of the Boston
and New York City marathons

Sales is like dating. When you first see each other you both form an instant opinion. Instantly you have the chance to create a terrific first impression if you desire.

Let's think about an interview situation. You and three other candidates are in the lobby waiting to be interviewed. The interviewer walks around the corner to view all four of you even if she will interview only one at a time. Do you look like the person she wants to hire?

I remember being the interviewer for one-person-at-a-time interviews and I could tell pretty fast if a sales candidate had a chance to make it.

Now, there are definitely prospects (the 1 percent) who do not fit any mold, but can sell. I found them by talking to them. They would immediately create a superior impression and exhibit a tenacious attitude. When I think back to my own first set of job interviews, I remember telling the sales manager I would start out at the top of the John Hancock Center (in downtown Chicago) and would cold call every business in the building. If no one bought, I would start at the top again. I had no fear of rejection. He told me he would call me if he was interested. He called 15 minutes after I had left his office and told my mom I had the job if I wanted it.

There is only one way to deal with rejection. Don't think about it as a negative. We tend to believe that this works for muscles in a sports arena, but it is really the working of an athlete's mind. Offer your mind positive suggestions repeatedly and your mind will obey. You will have no preset rejection level.

Speaking of rejection recently I read about bars hosting speed dating events. You apply and fill out a form describing basic pertinent information concerning your personal and professional life. You are then matched with an assortment of people. You have 15 minutes to make a positive impression on the other person so you have a chance for a future date. EEEEERRRRRRR! Times up.

I think this could just as easily be completed in five minutes. I would choose a five-minute window of time and request to see three times as many prospective partners. I would simply ask as many questions as possible in the time allotted.

Here's another related anecdote. When Sting, the ex-Police Sting (like you know another Sting) was single, he would approach women by asking them for change. Jay Leno confessed that when he dated girls who owned cats he would rub catnip on his shirt buttons. Now if Sting and Jay both need a gimmick, I think we should all review our methods.

I want you to stop reading, look up from the page and describe yourself. Then write it down._____

Now I want you to describe your firm to a prospective client. Write it down._____

Okay, now keep reading.

At EVCOR, I would ask all new sales candidates to describe EVCOR at our first interview. One of my first questions was, "How would you describe EVCOR to a new client who had never heard of us before?"

All new candidates had researched EVCOR on the Internet. They had viewed our web site and knew a lot about our firm before I ever met them.

Invariably they would describe it like a surgeon depicting a tumor on a lung.

I would ask the candidate if they would do business with our firm instead of the competitor based on their description. They always said, "Probably not." Their description always stated exactly what EVCOR did. Something like this was a normal response. "EVCOR sells mailing and shipping systems. It is headquartered in Aurora, Illinois. It offers sales and service."

I would always say, "Want to learn how to describe things so people want to buy them?" They would say yes and I would describe EVCOR like this: "EVCOR is the largest independent competitor to Pitney-Bowes (PB) and Friden/Alcatel in the

United States. EVCOR is an Inc. 500 award winner with an outstanding 1,019 percent growth rate and ranked the ninth fastest growing company in Illinois. We are number 1 in integrated PC-to-mainframe shipping systems saving you millions of keystrokes per year. Our software based systems facilitate the shipping of boxes for Intel, GE, Abbott Labs, Sony Oracle, and 3,000 other customers."

I would finish and then ask the candidates if this sounded cool. They always answered yes and our interview continued.

I am a huge fan of "you are who you hang with." Insert some of your best-known customers' names with your first impression description and watch your sales climb. Most people six months out of college know PB and Friden/Alcatel are huge firms so my reps always compared our smaller firm to them. It made us appear bigger in the eyes of the prospect.

Energize your opening statement by sprinkling in brand name references and unique corporate achievements. Researchers have discovered that a person viewing Internet web sites can determine in 50 milliseconds whether they like the site. That is $1/20^{th}$ of a second. How long do you think it takes a prospect to determine if you are worth the time when you begin with a lame opening statement or are not dressed appropriately?

Initial Reaction versus Fact

You are not better than anyone else but no one is better than you.
My dad, David J. Evans

My father was a first lieutenant in the Army Corps of Engineers during World War II. One of the duties he had was to train recruits in hand-to-hand combat. "What if ..." was constantly in his vocabulary.

One story, which has stuck with me, is the "dog attack defense." Let me ask you a question. What would you do if a Doberman Pinscher was 20 yards away and started running at you with his mouth frothed? I have asked many salespeople this same question. The answer is always the same. "I would run," the reps have all answered. I then explain that the crazed four-legged dog is at least twice as fast as you. Next, I ask the reps, "What part of your body would the dog bite first?" "My leg," most of them say and a few volunteered their "butt."

I then would explain how my dad taught me to fend off a dog in an attack.

"Stand your ground, bend your legs, and assume a fight stance," he said. "If you are right-handed you jab your left arm out in front of you and dangle your left hand. The onrushing beast will attack the first piece of you it detects. When the dog lunges at your left hand, you time it and then yank your left hand back at the exact moment you thrust your right fist into the dog's nose."

This will stop the dog in its tracks.

I know it sounds tough but once you realize your original RUN defense is dumb, maybe hitting the dog's nose sounds better. I bet you every cell in your body wants you to RUN but that will invite disaster. The dog will attack, bite you, drag you down … well, you get the picture.

In sales you sometimes face a "fight-or-flight" situation but it is disguised as a "hold your price/drop price" scenario. The pressure can be enormous. Hold your price and ask a question.

Do you want to please people or sell product?

Whenever I interviewed new sales reps, they would invariably state they were a people person or they liked people. I would always respond, "Great, are you hungry?" They would get flustered and then recover with, "What do you mean?"

Sales managers should hire hungry reps, people who have something to prove. Every interviewee likes people or they would not be on a sales interview. They may subconsciously think a sales career is beneath them. Don't hire these people.

The reason I relate the dog attack story to new reps is I want them to experience their initial reaction as being flawed. I train sales reps by peeling away their wrong assumptions and role-playing correct assumptions, which become a part of their successful persona.

There is a huge difference between pleasing people and selling prospects. See the difference already? I call them prospects and you call them people. I view meetings as negotiations and you may view them as conversations. Big difference.

Part V
ORGANIZING

21-Day Challenge

SM: You sailed in two Olympic regattas. In 1964 you won a bronze in the FD then returned to win gold in the Soling in 1972. How were these two experiences different and how were they the same?

Melges: Mind-set. In 1964 the goal was to get to the Olympics. In 1972 the goal was to go and win a gold medal. In short, setting goals and training to and for those goals made the difference. Having the experience of the 1964 games also helped in containing [our] emotions with all the "hoopla" surrounding the games.
Sailing Medalist interviewing Harry "Buddy" Melges Jr.

You can achieve a 30-day sales quota in 21 days. It takes 21 days to break a habit but if you don't know what positive actions to perform for 21 days, you screw up even worse. I like to think of it as 21 days to migrate over to a new approach instead of "break" or "change." When you migrate you move from one place to another in a deliberate motion. Birds migrate ever year and they seem to make it down south in one piece. Twenty-one days gives you time to absorb the lessons necessary for you to achieve your personal goals every month. Let's migrate together and achieve.

I lay out a 21-day plan for you. Follow it and you will be successful. The #1 element in being a success is your attitude. Remember when your parents would suggest, "You had better change your attitude and we mean NOW!" Well, NOW is now.

Let me tell you a secret. Every successful sales rep has "gears." Each gear has a unique mind-set. We each have four gears based on a 30-day sales quota cycle.

1. Days 1–7.   The first week

2. Days 8–14.   The second week

3. Days 15–21.   The third week

4. Days 22–31.   The fourth week

First gear is utilized in the first week. You have to get started up the hill of a new month. If you wait until Monday morning you are lost. Start on Saturday and plan your next month's activities. On Sunday review the plan and decide what time you need to wake up, what you are wearing, whether you are starting at your office or at a prospect's location and check the traffic/weather report on the Internet.

On Monday your head must be totally into the present moment. You should burst on the scene and be in full-fledged battle gear by 7:15 A.M. The first business days are relegated to tying up any loose strings from closed deals in the previous month. Start making cold calls to new prospects and select current customers to call who may need to make a change. Note that I did not say "want" I said "need." Closers look for blood in the water.

On days 3 to 7 you mix some cold calls in with some contacts to present customers. What is the difference between a present customer needing versus wanting to acquire your product or service? A terrific example is my very first completed sale, which occurred within months of graduating from college. I cold called a present customer who owned a postage machine base from Singer/Friden but leased the postage meter on top of the base. I walked in and discovered that the travel agency was abusing the meter equipment. Our policy clearly stated hand crank meters could not process over $50 per month in postage. The customer's logbook showed postage purchased averaging over $150 per month. I (gulp) asked to see the office manager and informed them that they had to upgrade to a more heavy duty meter and signed them on the spot. They needed to make a decision.

Your competition is involved in the same need situations on their side of the tracks. The main idea of cold calling is you attempt to find your competitor's customers at the end of the sales cycle. The idea is to weed out the deals the competition is just about to close.

Week one does not have urgency attached to it. Similar to a basketball game, the first quarter is where the teams feel each other out.

Second gear entails days 8 to 14. The weekend was a blast and you found time on Saturday and Sunday to plan your next week with an emphasis on planning Monday (the first day). Warning: If you don't take the time on Sunday night to plan, then Monday will streak by and become Monday night faster than you can mumble, "What happened to Monday?" Nonquota attaining sales reps actually lose 50 percent of their Mondays every week. Not a good plan.

This second week should be great for you. Second gear kicks in and you are euphoric. The stress of weeks three and four are in the future and you are now one week removed from last month. Increase the raw number of cold calls each day now. Place a mirror in front of you on your desk and dial for dollars. The mirror trick I learned from a copier company called Altman Copiers. It allows you to perform many more cold calls without getting bored or depressed since you actually see yourself smiling and selling. Your mission this week is to call as many noncustomers as you can for 75 percent of each day. You are similar to an athlete on a beach with an extrasensitive metal detector. You run down the beach fast and if the detector BEEPS, you stop and start selling.

The two easiest prospects to sell are (1) your own customers who have a need and (2) your competitor's customers who are being forced to purchase because of a perceived need.

I was in our Madison, Wisconsin, branch office years ago and one of my sales reps said she was proceeding to sign a deal but the customer wouldn't sign until the first week of next month. ALARM BELLS were set off in my head when I heard this. I asked her, "Why not this month?" The rep had no explanation so I called the lady who was head of purchasing for the respective firm. She explained to me how much she liked our rep and ... I listened and then asked if we could entice her to sign today. That is when she stunned me with, "Oh, we are signing with your competitor this afternoon." Her name was Beverly so I asked, "Beverly, why would you sign with them?" She told me the rep had set a deadline date because his prices were increasing the next month. I drove over to her office and closed her within one hour.

Wednesday and Thursday of the second week are very productive. You will see more good leads develop in this sweet spot than any other time. Friday's production depends on the season. If it is summer you should start work 30 minutes earlier than normal because you will lose people toward the end of the day. And you can compensate for this loss.

Days 16 to 21 represent Close Week. Most nonquota generating salespeople think the best week is week four. It's not. It's the third week.

Third gear is awesome to behold. In every major sales contest I've been in I won in the third week. The other sales reps get psyched out because my volumes are so high one week before the month closes. Here is what you should do. On Saturday or Sunday plan this week down to the minute. Monday arrives and you should have your first appointment at a prospect's office or in your conference room if all closable suspects are in attendance.

You are now a machine. In week one you gathered prospects together. During week two you massaged these potential leads and drilled down to find more exact needs. Week three is where you close all your deals.

Write it down!

21 days + you = Success

My dad always taught me to find the top person and ask them how they achieved success. "How long did it take you?" My dad then told me to cut that time frame in half. My goal was then set. Sell as much as the top person in one-half the time. My dad recognized that if I did not hit my numbers I would still set a record.

If you follow the steps you will achieve a 30-day quota in 21 days. Once you have achieved this there is no going back. You will have programmed yourself and you will top quota consistently. Ross Perot of EDS and Perot Systems actually hit his annual sales quota for IBM in the first month during one of the years he was with them. WHOA!

Sell Like You Are a Business

Breakthrough TV commercial that describes a typical American family and how they view themselves as a stock pick.

John Hancock Insurance TV ad

I recently received a letter from an investment broker. He wanted to manage my portfolio and enclosed some information regarding his investment philosophy. His basic strategy to help me achieve my overall financial goals was included.

The firm wanted to develop a personalized plan for me that would help remove any guesswork and emotion. I started to imagine pie charts and graphs demonstrating in excruciating detail how I could achieve financial security.

Then it hit me. Wealthy people always utilize these organizational tools. Once you achieve a high net worth, you are forced to diversify in an attempt to reach two goals. First, you want to protect the money you already own. Second, you want your money to generate more money.

Why don't neophyte sales reps utilize these tools? If they did, they would simply follow a path to wealth. Humor me and follow this four-step personal investment philosophy process:

1. Define your time and money objectives and risk tolerance.

2. Develop a suitable asset allocation.

3. Recommend an appropriate time and money investment strategy.

4. Monitor your plan to insure ongoing success.

When I talk to sales reps, I always remind them that each one of them is a business. Most of us live our lives according to a set 12-month schedule. December ends the year and January starts the new year. I have yet to meet an aggressive rep who has no borrowings. When he/she purchases a house or condo, a mortgage is usually part of the package. Newsflash—a mortgage is debt. You miss the payments and the banker takes your home.

You better keep score if you want to grow your net worth. You may have a partner (spouse) and interested parties (kids). Sure sounds like a business to me. Let's start.

Define Your Time and Money Objectives and Risk Tolerance

You are not only a business but I can prove you run a seasonal business.

1. How much money (net of taxes) do you have to meet your personal financial commitments per year?

    Expenses per year? _____ /12 months _____ /4 weeks _____ /5 days

The reason I choose to show four weeks (one month) and each day is this: It gives you a road map of exactly how much money you need to bring in per day or at the end of the month to exceed your expenses.

2. How many hours per year can you guarantee to be selling? Selling does not include training or being at the office, unless you are cold calling, or in front of a prospect. It does not include typing a quote or preparing for a demonstration. You sell during the day and after 5 P.M. you complete any paperwork or input.

Selling hours per year? _____ /12 months _____ / 4 weeks _____ 5 days

Please locate a writing pad. Down the left-hand column I want you to list any expense categories utilizing every other line. Examples are gas, food, clothing, utilities, mortgage payments, and so on. Along the top, from left to right, please list the months of the year (January to December). Leave one open column to the right for totals. You can also produce this graph on a spreadsheet. (See Figure 27.1.)

The expenses for Figure 27.1 can be found in your checkbook and credit card statements. The graph will illuminate your seasonal cash flow needs. It will illustrate your largest expenditures and when they occur. Now you know how much cash you need to exceed your expenses per month.

Be a fanatic about your time. Protect it. Am I proposing to limit your time talking to fellow sales reps? Yes, I am. Partake in conversations with a quick joke or a fast story, and then get back to selling. Pick up the phone and call a prospect.

	Jan	Feb	Mar	Apr	May	Jun	Jul	Aug	Sep	Oct	Nov	Dec	TOTALS
Gas	$												$
Food	$												$
Clothing	$												$
And so on	$												$
TOTALS	$$$												$$$

Figure 27.1 Expense Spreadsheet

If you were in the middle of a live presentation to an existing customer, would you talk to a fellow employee and joke around? No, you wouldn't. So the faster you become successful, the less you have to worry about this conundrum.

Don't get me wrong. Every single person I ever worked with will gladly tell you they like me and they never noticed that I didn't small talk. I love to talk. I would just quickly comment between phone calls. I would tell a story on the way to or back from the men's room, but I guarded every second of every single day. I sold.

Once you feel the high of achieving a sale, you want to feel it again and again. You have been told you are trusted, you are liked, and you are efficient. Not a bad high.

The same advice goes for cold calling door-to-door. The UPS (United Parcel Service) delivery people run from their trucks to the customer's door. Why? In one eight-hour day, the UPS driver saves X number of minutes. Run to your next prospect. Okay, okay, you can start by walking faster toward your next prospect.

Develop a Suitable Asset Allocation

What Are Your Financial Assets?

- Your time?
- Your car?
- Your home?
- Your savings?

How much time each day can you work? Can you miss quota and still meet your home and car payments? I believe you should maximize your workday and put in at least 11-hour days to jump-start your sales career.

Recommend an Appropriate Time and Money Investment Strategy

- *Your time.* Account for every 15-minute segment from 7:30 A.M. until at least 7:30 P.M. After 21 days you no longer have to account for this.

- *Your car.* Group your presentations and closes together geographically so you save gas and time. Once you have an appointment set for a certain day, simply schedule the next appointment in the vicinity.

- *Your home.* Achieve quota so you can enjoy more time with your family. If you don't achieve quota your work may become more stressful, affecting your home life. You cannot achieve in sales and be home by 5 P.M. each night.

- *Your savings.* Interview three investment brokers and select one to seek advice from. Do this early in your sales career.

Monitor Your Plan to Insure Ongoing Success

- *Your time.* The first action I want you to take is multiply your monthly quota by 1.5. If you attempt to achieve this new higher quota amount and come up short, you will still hit quota. This works. I had a sales rep in Chicago who continually missed quota. I boosted his quota by 1.5 and he started hitting actual quota within two months.

Let me relate a terrific sales story David Jones, the former president of Bell & Howell, told me. He used to eat lunch in the corporation's cafeteria with the troops. He sat down next to a sales rep and started asking him questions about his territory. The rep complained he could not reach quota because of how spread out his customer base was. David grabbed a napkin and drew a square and labeled it YOUR TERRITORY. He then drew a line down the middle and told the sales rep he had solved the rep's problem. David had cut the territory in half. The rep was stunned but it was a great sales lesson. I presumed the rep had an easier time hitting quota with his customers now being so close.

Add 15 minutes to each day. No matter how many hours you now put into work simply add 15 minutes more to every day. This is the best way to guarantee your success versus that of previous months. It will actually produce 62.5 more hours per year or an additional week per year of sales time. You can work longer hours or delete 15 minutes from your personal (non-business) tasks throughout each day.

On Sunday night, review your upcoming sales week. Do not allow anyone or anything to divert you from selling during the week. If you identify a diversion write it down or place it in your PDA (personal digital assistant).

- *Your car.* Review your past week each Sunday night. I presume you plan each day the night before and this will make sense of your entire week. If you have not been geographically grouping your presentations you must notice it and start doing it.

- *Your home.* If you have an adjustable rate mortgage check to see if you can conserve cash by locking into a long-term interest rate. You may need to refinance if rates dip. The rule of thumb for refinancing is if you can shave 2 percentage points off and you plan to stay in your home for at least two more years it is probably the right move.

- *Your savings.* Monitor your money market account, CD, and so on, minimally once per month. Fill out a personal financial statement at least once per year so you have a scorecard of success or failure financially. This is extremely important. Don't do this and you are programming your subconscious mind to ignore the score-keeping goal-oriented mind-set. Warning: You cannot fool the goal-oriented mechanism inside your brain.

Financial security for my family was my goal as a sales rep. I've achieved that goal and so can you.

Write it down!

Organizing

You are a seasonal business. You will guarantee yourself in writing to sell for____hours this year. You will perform ___ presentations this year.

Run. Squeeze as many contacts into each day as possible. Make a game of it.

Start Up Capital?

A reporter once asked Mark Twain (Samuel Clemens) what was his definition of a sale. He responded, "That's simple. It's the difference between lightning and lightning bug."

What do you think he meant? The answer is easy to understand if you write it down. LIGHTNING—LIGHTNING BUG. The answer is BUG. The difference is one word. He meant you had to think, because you could gain or lose a sale with one word.

My favorite quote.

Anyone who has ever created a new business has worried about start-up capital. Where do I get it? How much do I need?

I have always preached that the best way to access start-up capital is to ask your future customers. If you are beginning an enterprise that offers customers continuing maintenance on software, equipment, or services then having the customer participate in helping you will work.

At EVCOR we offered one-year maintenance contracts on mailing machines. Our competition charged full price and collected the entire maintenance agreement 120 days in advance of the start date. So I sold prospects on switching to EVCOR's maintenance agreement to save 30 percent and we would invoice and collect 120 days in advance of the commencement date. This meant we could estimate our venture's first 12 months' costs and subtract those costs from the dollars we would receive from each paid maintenance agreement customer. If we sold enough MAs (maintenance agreements) we were "in like Flynn."

We would grow the company with the 120-day start-up money and then show up on the first day of the contract to introduce our technician to the mail machine operators.

Wouldn't we run out of money to service the customer properly toward the end of the MA? That never occurred even though I figured some customers would eat up more service time and expense than others. It seems maintenance contracts are very profitable and most firms sell them to make money. The customer likes them because they can budget their expense and hedge against unexpected major financial outlays.

Every sales rep should think of himself as an entrepreneur who is starting up a business. Every month you start with minimal capital to spend on the business. Funding? You have to close deals to keep capital coming in. The easiest firm to close is a present customer and the easiest product to close is a maintenance contract. If you sell an intangible then select the smallest, lowest cost item a new account can purchase and go for it.

Quit thinking like a protected salesperson who sells only certain items and think like an entrepreneur. Get a foothold on the beach. Forget about "thinking outside the box" and sell the BOX or better yet, lease the space the box is sitting on.

Go into your territory and visit the biggest accounts that do NOT do business with you. Sell them on purchasing a minuscule item that your firm handles. This will get you listed as a vendor in their computers and will allow you to use their name as a reference. I once sold IBM a discounted six-pack of postal tape just so I could call on a separate department and say I already did business with IBM. Within six months their entire mailroom was mine.

I love home runs but singles and doubles win baseball games. Schedule one day (SINGLES DAY) when you visit the prospects just mentioned and close on small stuff. Do this one day per month and I guarantee you that a large deal will surface from one or more of the accounts. Why? You are visiting AND selling large accounts that do not do biz with you now. These same accounts purchase all the time. Trust me on this one. It's a small numbers game that builds exponentially.

It is similar to the successful technique I teach new sales reps when they have to find a parking space in downtown Chicago when every space is taken. Most drivers continually drive around the block and keep missing spaces that get filled just before they get to the space. Don't drive around in circles. Find the longest row of parked cars and pull over. Someone will leave within four minutes and you will be poised to see them pulling out before anyone else does.

Write it down!

So start your new biz (in your territory if you are a rep) and remember to call 1-800-THE-CUSTOMER-WILL-FRONT-ME-THE-MONEY.

Six Degrees from Kevin Bacon

I told you I was sick.

My favorite gravestone inscription (given to me by
Terry Lee who owned a cemetery monument business)

Have you ever played the movie celebrity game "Six Degrees from Kevin Bacon?" It was inspired by the stage play *Six Degrees of Separation*. You get six chances to tie the actor, Kevin Bacon, to another movie actor, through movies, mutual directors, fellow celebrities, and so on. It is amazing how adept people are in achieving this. An example that took only four moves is: Morgan Freeman (actor), *Million Dollar Baby* (movie Freeman acted in), Clint Eastwood (acted and directed *Million Dollar Baby*), *Mystic River* (directed by Clint Eastwood), Kevin Bacon (acted in *Mystic River*).

Well, when you are selling it is very important to tie your prospect into your known network. An example of this is discovering the names of the directors at your prospect's firm. Then you can find out the name of the firm each particular director works for. Cross-reference the firm with your existing customer base and if you locate any matches, you have a tremendous reference account your prospect will be interested in since it is "so close to home." A director is seen as a trusted advisor. If his or her firm likes your product, then you have a trusted reference. BA-DA-BING!

You can retrieve the names and firms of the board of directors simply by entering in "board of directors for _____ (fill in corporate name)" in a search engine like Google.

How can you access even more info on your prospect for free? Well, you can enter Hoovers.com and retrieve very valuable information for no cost. It is a division of Dun & Bradstreet (D&B) and it covers a lot of territory.

1. Enter hoovers.com into a search engine and then click

2. RESEARCH, or

3. Type in the company name.

4. Click on the company's legal name from the choices presented.

You will view the key facts:

- Public or privately held.
- Fiscal year end (so you can close quickly if their year end is impending).
- Annual sales $.
- 1 year sales growth (Are they growing?).
- # of employees. (Divide the annual sales $ by the number of employees to achieve a productivity $ figure. Compare this to three of the competitors you will find on hoovers.com. Any answer close to or less than $100,000 is not great.)

The best references can be found within your prospect.

Write it down!

Seek the link.

Researchers have informed us that any one human is only a few generations removed from all other humans. We share a link and your job is to exploit that fact.

Bring home the Bacon with SalesBURST!!

Part VI
SHOWING

Trade Shows: A Successful Way to Sell From a Booth

Skate to where the puck is going to be.
Wayne Gretzky (NHL Hall of Famer)

Selling from a business show booth can be intimidating. "Are you working the show?" If you answer affirmatively, then this sales tip will make you money.

I learned this sales lesson from a tall, lanky, laid-back business associate who lived in Atlanta. He was a quiet guy who had a hard time walking up to strangers and starting a conversation. To combat his insecurity he created a wonderful way to meet new clients while working a booth at a business show.

The problem with prospects is they walk down the middle of the aisle very fast just glimpsing each booth. Aggressive sales reps yell to the prospect usually eliciting a smile and a faster walking prospect.

My friend taught me to walk very slowly toward the prospect with one piece of literature in my left hand which is hanging by my side. Prospects will always take the lit from you just to get rid of you. When you approach the prospect, raise your arm with the literature as if you want to hand it to his/her right hand. The prospect will assume it is the usual "take the lit and keep walking" routine but just before the prospect grabs the lit you drop your left arm down, raise your right arm (at the same time) and shake the prospect's outstretched hand.

Now you are shaking hands so please ask a question. The one I asked was, "Hi, does your firm ship with UPS?" I asked this because any purchasing agent, IT manager, or mid-to-upper level exec would know the answer. If the answer was yes I then turned toward my booth and walked in unison with the prospect to the booth.

The question simply predetermines what level of prospect you have in front of you. Most any question works but the best ones are very simple and receive a yes. This worked every time I tried it. I have executed it thousands of times and it works for quiet, nonaggressive, as well as type A sales reps. With this method you feel no pressure and you always end up talking to tons of prospects.

You can attain your goals. So BURST from your shell and go shake hands and start selling.

Write it down!

You can sell even if you are a laid-back individual. You may not be an assertive personality type and that's fine. I've trained many sales reps who became terrific sales talents using a more relaxed two-step approach. Simply emulate what an assertive person does but do it in two steps.

When cold calling a receptionist in the mailing industry, an assertive rep will simply walk up and say, "I'm here concerning the mailing machine." The receptionist can assume you are there to fix a possibly broken machine or she can ask who you are with. Believe it or not your odds are 45 percent that she will allow you to start walking toward the mailing machine without asking any questions.

A less-assertive rep will stop at the desk and ask for the correct spelling of the purchasing manager's name and her phone number. The receptionist will give this info out and the rep then will call the firm later but will sound very convincing since the manager is being asked for by name instead of title.

More Booth Marketing Ideas

You sail on the edge of controllability.
Paul Cayard (America's Cup and Olympic racing sailor)

My philosophy has always been to make money without spending a lot of money.

When I started EVCOR, I worked out of my house for a year and a half. I was forced to relocate after the Downers Grove, Illinois, police got wind of my 800-square-foot garage chock full of electronic scales and mailing machine remanufacturing parts. They accused me of running a business out of my house. What?

I moved my administrative functions to a very small office and continued the garage element for six more months. The police must have listened to that old Bob Dylan song about the fired lumberjack in the Northwoods because "one day the axe just fell."

With the profits I saved from eliminating rent, I purchased a 2,500-square-foot building with a built-in 500-square-foot loft. My fledgling firm utilized every square inch. The building was sold to me by a sales and loan institution, whose president had the name Crook (no kidding), who absconded with their profits. I sold that building within three years and pocketed $200,000. Forget being Hooked on Phonics, I was hooked on real estate.

EVCOR started reaching out and growing into other states. We started attending business shows targeted toward UPS shipping and USPS (let's go postal) mailing.

Visit any show where sales reps hawk their products and/or services. What do you see? Probably lots of people hopefully walking up and down aisles. Are they looking up or down? Most prospects look at your booth and the booth across the aisle, while they are 30 feet away and then look down when they get close to you. They do not want to make eye contact since that could imply interest on their part. EVCOR taped cardboard signs with advertising to the carpet in front of our booth. Yes, I know we shouldn't, but we did.

We also dressed all the sales reps in costumes. My favorite was the PB ON TRIAL booth, where every rep was draped in black judge's robes. Some even got into it and wore powered white wigs emulating England's barristers.

EVCOR sold and serviced computerized shipping systems and remanufactured mail machines, so I placed two mail machines on the front table of the 10 × 10 booth and hung a sign that asked, WHICH MACHINE IS NEW? The competition's vice-president selected one and was wrong just like many other prospects. You see, they were both remanufactured and they both looked brand new. If a prospect was interested, but wouldn't commit we would offer a short on-site trial. We had a gas at that show.

One idea to notate is where the best location for a 10 × 10 booth is. Review the show's prospectus and find where your largest competitor is located. Is it near the front doors? You can compete if you use your head. Usually prospects walk down the first aisle or the center aisle. Place your booth at the very end of a long aisle against the wall. Prospects will view it every time they turn and walk around to continue the show.

Most booths utilize bright colors. You should utilize black and white. It cuts through the clutter and allows you to be seen and remembered. Hang a huge sign behind your booth with a catchy phrase using white letters on a stark black background. Hang a second smaller sign on the front of the booth with an invitation announcing something akin to TAKE THE MAILING MACHINE CHALLENGE.

Another guerrilla booth idea is to locate the booth across from the public cafeteria. This affords a small booth much more exposure and allows prospects who are eating lunch to sit and stare at your message.

A successful strategy we experimented with was having two 10 × 10 booths in different areas of the show. It never failed to stun me when we reviewed the leads and found very little overlap.

Another very successful booth was Ghost Busters. Right after the movie came out we had an important show in Chicago. A few days before the show, I got the idea to dress all the sales reps in white lab coats with green slime on them. My wife and I hung the lab coats on lines in the backyard and sprayed them with green slime. Everyone stopped at the booth.

A cardboard sign was placed on the carpet in front of the booth and all it had on it were two imprints of feet painted in incandescent orange. I had witnessed these same feet at Disney World. People from all over the world recognize this as the international equivalent of "stand here."

We coincidentally positioned our booth directly across from the competition's booth. Prospects would walk up and stand on the feet, but face the competitor's booth. We would place reverse mirror sunglasses on the prospects (these cost like $1) and would ask, "What interest rate are you being charged on your mail machine base lease?"

We would then tell them to read the answer, which was printed on a huge sign in the back of our booth. Remember, even though the prospect was facing the competitor's booth they could see our booth clearly because of the reverse mirrors in the sunglasses. They would say the interest rate (which was very high) and one of our reps with a small bullhorn would scream the answer to the show participants. Boy, I miss that booth.

Write it down!

Exercise aggressive techniques when designing your show booths. Go bland and receive bland results. Want word of mouth advertising where people at the show create the buzz? Go black and white and excite.

SalesBURST!! homework is to design one unique show booth per year to test my theories. Call me when the leads pour in.

Part VII
MARKETING

FREe-commerce

Me? Whee!!
Muhammad Ali (world heavyweight boxing champion
delivers the shortest poem ever written to
Harvard's graduating class in 1975)

FREe-commerce was an idea that came to me during the heyday of the Internet e-commerce explosion. Our sales force needed a way to simplify the process of e-commerce for suppliers and manufacturers. E-commerce represented the elimination of paper-based order processing. It permitted:

- One firm to place an order.
- Another firm to acknowledge the receipt of that order, send a change order if out of stock, create and transmit an advance ship notice, and process an e-payment after an electronic invoice was received.

The labor savings were astronomical so every prospect wanted the benefits. Two issues needed to be dealt with before we could capitalize on the huge pentup demand in this marketplace.

The first issue was that a prospect needed to face the changes that would occur if their company implemented the solution. People are very afraid of change even if their present solution is inadequate. We could deal with that by educating the prospect's employees and offering satisfied references from early adopters of the software.

The second issue was, as they say, "stickier." Manufacturers and large trading partners had the money to pay for the efficiencies demonstrated in the system but refused to pay for the smaller suppliers to be brought online because they represented only 20 percent of the revenues to the large firms. It was the old 80/20 principle in action. The suppliers were ubiquitous but they elicited many small dollar orders. The manufacturers communicated with their large suppliers utilizing an ancient technology termed EDI (electronic data interchange). It was proprietary, cost a fortune to install, processed all transactions through a virtual toll booth that charged per transaction and worked well enough that it was hard to displace.

Our solution utilized a newer technology coined XML (extensible markup language), a sister technology to HTML (hypertext markup language), which you are very familiar with if you have ever viewed any web site. The main difference between the sister technologies was XML could be sent between computers with no human intervention, allowing extremely fast processing of data and seemingly a perfect environment for exploiting the huge e-commerce market of nonconnected suppliers. XML was low cost, nonproprietary, and levied no transaction charges.

The manufacturers and large hubs would love to eliminate the labor associated with faxed orders sent to them by the smaller suppliers because their people would have to manually type each transmission into the host computer. This represented a slow and error prone process distasteful to the big guys but again the bulk of the dollars coming into the large members of this trading community were already automated.

Let's review that scenario. Big members want to eliminate labor and will not spend money to automate small trading partners. Small partners do not possess the mind-set to pay for automation and will continue to use slow, laborious manual methods until forced to comply by the larger partner. The suppliers were not about to sign and pay for a long-term commitment of monthly payments when they felt the larger partner reaped the economic benefits. We were not going to offer trials or guarantee that the supplier would enjoy trading electronically since that was subjective. I do not know how this next phrase entered our lexicon but this appeared to be a Mexican standoff and I was being positioned as a possible piñata.

I studied the scenario, placed all my options on paper, and waited for an answer to materialize. Three days later I just happened to notice an ad for a firm called U-promise. Their premise utilized a FREE concept and was pitched to all the AOL (America Online) customers over the Internet. The plan enabled people with children who will attend college in the future to pay for their kids' education by receiving discounts from third parties. U-promise signed automakers like GM, gasoline distributors like Shell, grocery stores like Jewel and Dominick's and so on, so literally a percentage of every dollar the parents spent in their normal daily lives would be forced into a trust account, which took advantage of recent college tuition savings plans. The plan's simplicity was brilliant and many celebrities and top government officials backed it.

It appeared to be all based on a very simple flaw in human character. If all parents of future college grads simply set aside a percentage of their earnings U-promise may not have ever existed. The sad truth is parents are not saving in government-shielded accounts for their kids' impending college tuition costs. Ask them and they will reply they desire to save but they also want vacations and luxury items that have turned their heads and demagnetized their parental responsibility compass.

What if we could create FREe-commerce?

What if we could have a third party pay for our prospects' e-commerce software and implementations? Then the answer jumped off the page! We would make a list of items that our prospects, America's suppliers, purchased to run their respective businesses. The suppliers would need certain items but what would all the suppliers need? They all order and use office supplies was the only answer that appeared plausible. So I decided to perform some basic math calculations that guaranteed our firm $750 per year from each supplier. If we needed to receive this dollar amount each year, how much would each supplier have to spend on office supplies annually to guarantee a sufficient gross margin to the large office supply firm? I inserted a gross margin of five percent since I heard this was the usual margin the office supply industry survived on. Therefore the annual dollar amount that a supplier needed to purchase from one of the huge office supply retailers was $18,000.

If we could locate suppliers who already purchased this dollar amount annually, and they were not present customers of the specific office supply firm we would utilize as our partner, then I could introduce the two firms and be paid the $750 portion from the office suppliers' profits.

It was a beautiful thing. My firm receives the $750 each year, the supplier receives a FREe-commerce software system with implementation, the office supply firm receives a new customer (while committing no up front market spending) and the manufacturer receives an electronic commerce enabled trading partner that saves them money by increasing efficiency and eliminating all keystroke errors prominent in the old faxed order, received and typed into the host computer methodology.

FREe allowed four partners to become more efficient, save money and grow their businesses.

Write it down!

The #1 issue in business is traction. Start selling and you will notice that your industry will change. *Traction* is defined as "adhesive friction." You want to start moving forward so you can be pulled instead of having to push for sales every month.

Once you start moving forward you will notice new ways to grow your customer base. Soon you will become competent at selling because you understand your product and how it fares against your competition. At this juncture you can attempt to branch out and make your product FREe by securing third party alliances.

The Special OFFER idea utilized in the marketing of Sales-BURST!! is a perfect example of the FREe marketing concept. How can you use the FREe idea to market your product?

Lease and Refinance

Chaos is infinitely complex order.

David Bohm, visionary physicist and author of
Wholeness and the Implicate Order.

1986 was a terrific year to refinance your house. Thousands of Americans cashed in on their home's rising equity. They shortened the length of their mortgage, built additions, or simply stuffed the bucks into their pockets. In fact so many refinancing deals were taking place that a cartoon appeared in a small local Downers Grove, Illinois, daily newspaper. It depicted a young boy in a tree house yelling down to his mom below, "Can we talk about refinancing?"

That night I was luxuriating in my nightly hot bath, which I gravitate toward, so I can wind down and fall into the arms of Morpheus, the god of dreams in Greek mythology. My eyes were closed and I could feel myself relaxing when it hit me. This idea was really big and I felt like a lightning bolt had seized me.

What if EVCOR could combat our competitor's strength in leasing by utilizing a "jujitsu" move? This would be equal to using a competitor's own weight against him in a fight. Our competitor charged exorbitantly high simple interest rates to their mail machine lease customers.

Still in the tub I screamed for Josie to please get a pad of paper, a pen, and a calculator. She knows the premium I place on speed in jotting down an idea. Benjamin Franklin always slept with writing materials next to his bed and so do I. Josie flew into the master bath and sat down. We would occasionally brainstorm together because it was so much fun. Oh, by the way, don't attempt nude SalesBURST!! thought until you can master it in casual business attire.

The idea was simple. EVCOR could locate our competitor's customers in our database and explain to them how much they were paying to keep their present mailing base. EVCOR could pay off the competitor's finance firm, have the customer sign over the rights of ownership of the machine base to us, and lower their monthly lease payment dramatically. Some of the customers elected to purchase the base and not refinance but others did not. Why? Because all postage meter manufacturers must rent their meters to the end user customers. Why own a postage meter base from a virtual monopoly that is utterly useless without the rented meter? If you switched meter firms you "took a bath" on the meter base purchase. EVCOR also included a mail scale in with our lease proposal. A free scale coupled with a refinanced mail machine base was now a reality.

The math worksheet included number of payments remaining, present dollar amount of each payment, purchase option and payoff, and sales person's commission. The customer's were ecstatic since they kept the same machine, were given a new scale, lowered their monthly payment, and received a savings of 40 percent on their maintenance.

The customer would exercise its purchase option with our competitor and then transfer the ownership of the meter base to EVCOR. We would reimburse the purchase option cost and lower the monthly payment, supply a new scale, and lower the maintenance cost.

Attempt to train your mind to look at successful trends in other industries and splice the math, which created the success, into your specific environment. Refinance your career.

Write it down!

Offer a leasing alternative to your prospects. Do you offer a financing option to your prospects so they don't have to pony up the entire purchase price? You should because prospects think just like you. No one wants to spend money.

You can close deals faster if you prove to your future customer that the savings per day are more than the cost per day.

Write down your product's retail price_____. Add tax if your state requires it to be included in the monthly charge _____.

Multiply this amount by a monthly lease factor. You can receive the factors from many leasing firms including GE. The answer: _____.

Now you have the monthly cost to the prospect. Can you save the prospect any labor costs? Go on-site and measure every movement and every keystroke the prospect now uses in their present process. Figure out how many hours per day this equates to. Subtract the number of hours your replacement system will need. Multiply this answer by the number of business days per year excluding holidays (estimate 225). It could be more if the firm works on Saturday or has double shifts.

Now multiply that number by the hourly fee the employee is paid.

If your cost to the prospect per day is less than the dollar amount saved per day in labor, you WIN a sale. Don't short-change the equation. Include any benefits into your computations. Take the hourly wage and multiply by 1.2 (20%) to figure the benefit costs a firm pays out.

CHAPTER
34

Your Presentations

*Happiness does not depend on outward things
but on the way we see them.*

Leo Tolstoy

My sales career was like a rocket ship ride where I achieved top sales rep status in a downtown territory and then a suburban territory. I became a sales supervisor (which allowed me to manage three reps plus make a full commission on my territory sales), then sales manager, and finally a business owner. This all occurred within six years.

My very first home run was referred to as The 52 Envelopes. Like all my others ideas I tested it out myself before introducing it to other sales reps.

The firm I worked for, Friden, had introduced an electronic scale that sold for $6,175. We were supposed to sell this against our competitor's mechanical oil dashpot scale, which retailed for $395.

My sales force groaned when it heard the price difference but our electronic scale had unique and defined benefits, which demonstrated very well if a prospect would continue to listen after hearing the retail price.

I created The 52 Envelopes when my sales reps were repeatedly informed not to bother presenting the unit because the price was absurd.

The problems with the competitor's mechanical mail scale were numerous and if any one problem occurred, the scale would probably not weigh accurately.

First, I'll list the problems:

- *Low Oil*. Mechanical scales with low oil levels miscalculate scale weights.
- *Not Level*. The scale utilized a bubble leveler. If the bubble was not 100 percent covering its target then the scale was not level and would miscalculate.
- *Parallax Factor*. The mechanical scale had a faceplate with weights and postage rates printed on it. A thin line would sweep across the faceplate and stop in front of a weight/$. Depending on where the operator stood he/she could see straight or to the left or right. This is known as the parallax factor. The operator could easily misread the correct postage, which increased in one-ounce increments.
- *No Load Cell*. A mechanical scale weighs differently if a letter is half on and half off the platform.
- *Bounce*. Mail processors are forced to wait a second or two before finally reading the correct postage amount since mechanical dashpot scales could not settle immediately.

SalesBURST!!

The solution took advantage of all the competitor's scale deficiencies, exploited them, and made it fun for the prospect to view our presentation. Remember, selling is entertainment!

Now, I'll explain The 52 Envelopes solution. I set up a competitor's scale in our office and proceeded to place one envelope (with no contents) on the weighing platform. I then tore sheets of paper and placed them inside the envelope until the mechanical swing arm landed exactly dead center on two ounces. Sealing the envelope, I grabbed the next one.

The magic number was 52 because 52 envelopes fit into the cardboard container that the envelopes were sold in and we used it as a transport device. My sales force also thought 52 sounded scientific. Each envelope was loaded with a different weight and therefore the swing arm landed just to the left or right of each ounce most of the time.

Armed with the 52 envelopes, I grabbed a scale and a stopwatch and sped to my first cold call. Walking into a major mailroom in downtown Chicago, I announced to the mailroom manager that he was selected to see the newest technology in action. I requested his main mail processor to stand in front of his present mechanical scale and take The Test. Pulling out my stopwatch I made sure the processor saw it knowing full well he would think I was testing him for speed when I actually was testing him for accuracy. Simulating a very hectic mailroom atmosphere, which normally occurred between four and five o'clock, was critical because I wanted my sales reps to cold call with the scale throughout the entire day. The stopwatch worked its magic.

I pulled out a score sheet so I could write down the answers, which the mail processor would yell out. "Are we ready?" I would then yell, "GO!" The processor would grab an envelope, throw it on the mechanical scale, and yell the postage cost. He would tear that one off and slap the next one on (just like he was swamped with work and had to move fast to process all the mail before the final pickup deadline). It was terrific.

After 52 envelopes I would have him emulate these proceedings utilizing the electronic scale, which gave an instant correct postage rate no matter where the envelope was placed on the platform. When he was finished I sat down with the mailroom manager and showed him my score sheet. His firm would have lost $ _____ in those few minutes, and extrapolated over five years the loss was numbing.

I sold/leased three scales in the first two days and had created a pipeline of future leads. It was an unprecedented success. My sales force started performing the demos and our sales team proceeded to smash every sales record imaginable.

So what's the sales lesson here? Sales must be entertaining. Don't be boring. How can you explain the features and benefits of your product in a real time scenario so the prospect experiences what you believe is the problem and solution?

Not one mailroom manager turned down the cold call 52 Envelopes demo. Why? Curiosity wrapped in a 10-minute demonstration of new technology with no cost to the prospect. When they were told what the price was it was small compared to the phenomenal overpayments being made to the post office. We always quoted lease pricing when asked, "What's the price?" Then we compared the lease price per day to the savings per day.

My favorite memory of The 52 Envelopes was the stopwatch. The minute I displayed it you could see the race was on toward a sale.

Be creative. Have fun selling.

Write it down and an answer will appear. Review your product versus your competitor's. Feature versus Feature should expose the differences.

Is your presentation entertaining? If not, change it. People will remember the entertainment and want more, which means more of you. Entertaining does not have to translate to stand-up comedy. Interesting and insightful is great but strive for entertaining.

What is the best time of day to present your solution? You can perform relevant presentations all day long if you add a stopwatch type of angle.

CHAPTER
35

Good Medicine

Babies are born without kneecaps. They don't appear until the child reaches two to six years of age.

Things you didn't know you didn't know

How should you approach a sales opportunity in which you have to challenge the status quo? People do not like change so one way to make money is to convince them that they already allow what you are proposing. Even if you are not in the medical field the following example will inspire you to design a successful sales plan for your firm. Okay, here it is.

We are experiencing a healthcare crisis in America. Hospitals are losing money! Hospitals charge us more every year. How much more can we bear? If hospitals were more profitable, they could afford to charge us less. What if hospitals allowed advertising inside their premises?

This chapter deals with a real-life sales/marketing scenario. Some of America's hospitals are in dire shape and need money NOW. Hospitals are experiencing a severe nursing shortage and growing percentages are going out of business.

Scenario: To simply convince hospitals to place ads at the foot of the beds in the birthing recovery rooms. This is where entire families will experience the joy and miracle of welcoming a newborn baby. Remember, hospitals already allow advertising on the beds. They do? Keep reading.

Hospitals need new revenue streams to approach profitability. Industries are being challenged like never before. Post 9/11 airlines are now allowing advertising on pull-down trays, and so on. Why? They need more money just like our hospitals.

The Issues

- HIPAA (Health Insurance Portability and Accountability Act) went into effect April 14, 2003. "Hospitals could lose $3.5 billion in donations over the next 18 months," states the national fundraiser's trade group. Why? Target marketers are forbidden access so less effective mass mailings will have to be substituted.
- "Federal cutbacks in Medicare and Medicaid reimbursement rates have clobbered the hospitals ..." says David Broder, *Washington Post* Writers Group, in an article which appeared in the *Chicago Tribune*.

The Plan

"Adopt-a-bed": Offer third-party advertising appearing on clinical engineering's mobile assets (beds for example).

- Ads will appear approximately the same size as present manufacturer's logos appear. For example Hill-Rom (a major hospital supplier) places its name prominently at the foot of its beds. Next to the Hill-Rom name will appear a 3" × 7" ad paid for by an advertiser. It will be on a tan/beige label/sticker one shade different from Hill-Rom's present color. The label will be ordered from the same label manufacturer Hill-Rom presently utilizes. It will be able to be sterilized, washed, and disinfected. The label will stick to metal, stainless steel, or plastic and be able to be peeled off every half-year or year. The printing will appear black on a mat finish just like the Hill-Rom labels.

- NO COLOR ADS OR PICTURES WILL BE ALLOWED AND THE HOSPITAL CONTROLS WHOM IT WILL ALLOW TO ADVERTISE. IT COULD SIMPLY ALLOW THE NAME OF THE ADVERTISER AND NO ADDITONAL COPY.

Please remember the hospital already allows advertising. The correct question is does the hospital want to charge for the ads?

The Math

Newco (a fictitious firm) believes the hospital can place labels (ads) on the foot of each bed and reap huge financial benefits. If the hospital utilized all available beds it may have 215 beds × $1,400/year each (or $3.84/day ea.) = $301,000/yr. in new revenue.

Does $3.84/day sound like a lot of money to place an ad at the foot of the bed where every person who visits will certainly see it? Hill-Rom has this space now and pays nothing to the hospital.

This plan allows the hospital to have thousands of additional mobile assets (other than beds) to be able to sell ads on if it wishes.

The hospital could control the collection of ad revenues or it could outsource that function. The hospital would pay 20 percent of the ad revenues for 10 years to an outside firm who sells the ads and administrates the entire process. This would enable the hospital to keep a profit of $2,408,000 over 10 years.

The audience is family oriented and brings husbands and wives together with their kids. The typical visitor stays in the patient's room for one hour and always has time to view the different elements presented in the room. Hospitals are viewed with reverence in each community and already allow advertising—they just do not charge for it. Again, please view Hill-Rom beds and notice the size of Hill-Rom's name at the foot. Another manufacturer, Stryker, places its blue logo on the side rails. Check out some wheelchairs and view the manufacturer or distributor's name on each sidebar.

I believe the best matches have been banks, pharmaceutical firms, and so on. I recommend large brand name institutions that are well-known and conservative.

Have the hospital management look at one of the Hill-Rom beds or Stryker sidebars and they will smile and say, "We already allow brand advertising. Why aren't we charging for this?" I have tested this and that is what they do say.

This solution can bring $2,408,000 in ad revenue to the hospital's bottom line over the next 10 years if each bed simply has a label placed at its foot.

Write it down!

How can you convince a third party to pay money to your customers? Advertising is one surefire way. What do you think Google does? Google makes its revenues based on ad sales.

When I performed research for this chapter, I divided the market into two categories: healthy hospitals and unhealthy hospitals. I found that every level of management in the unhealthy hospitals I approached loved the idea. The healthy hospitals didn't need the revenue but most of the top management agreed they should think of charging for the ad space.

This example sells the advertising idea to the 75 percent of hospitals who need additional revenue and agree they already allow ads to be placed on equipment on their premises.

Review your customer base. Think outside the bed.

Better Than New

*If you don't make mistakes, you can't make decisions.
You can't dwell on them.*

Warren Buffett

One of the sales/marketing plans EVCOR successfully deployed was coined Better Than New. We considered it one notch away from our standard FREE plans.

EVCOR was growing like a weed on steroids when this story took place. We had a remanufacturing division that sold and leased preleased remanufactured mail machine bases.

We had taken over some larger volume accounts. One of these customers was the FNBC (First National Bank of Chicago), which was one of the largest volume mail houses in the entire Midwest. EVCOR referred to FNBC as a "billboard" account. We would always tell prospects EVCOR performed all the service for FNBC.

Life was great. Our business was running so smoothly and we were expanding so fast we did not notice the huge fan being moved into place. We did not observe the brown substance heading toward the fan. Then it happened! Our main competitor convinced FNBC to drop us and install NEW equipment. Our vice president of sales burst into my office and blurted, "First National is dropping us!"

I asked him a few pertinent questions to substantiate the competition's strategy and then proceeded to discuss avenues we could follow to fend them off. My father had taught me early on not to freak out during a crisis. I was trained to remain silent and use every ounce of strength to call up intelligence to thwart the adversary.

I started to jot down notes on a pad of paper. We have to make a counteroffer immediately, I thought. "What about First National's mailroom practices—their environment?" I asked. "Is there anything unique or unusual about how they process their mail that makes our solution better?"

My VP, who was now more relaxed, remembered they employed two massive 300-pound guys who pretty much ran the mailroom. Both guys wore huge elliptical Harley belt buckles. The reason this is pertinent is I remembered that FNBC's mail machines always looked all scratched up on the fronts facing the mailroom. Hmmm, let's see, the competitor is offering brand new equipment but the customer's mail personnel will gouge, scratch, and deface them the very first day.

I looked at my VP and opined, "What if we stop them by offering the bank a better than brand new solution?" I had always loved marketing type solutions where it sounded too good to be true. I had always tested crazy sounding ideas on my wife Josie who once in a while would respond, "You can't do that." What she had meant was the idea sounded so good that I probably could not make money and please the customer. These are the very ideas I would then put through the math paces to prove I could pull it off. If the equations backed me up then I would proceed (usually in total silence) to create an entire plan around it.

The math began to flow onto the page. We would strive to be slightly less than the price we presumed our competitor was quoting, but we would offer to replace our mail machine bases every 12 months at no additional cost to the bank for up to 36 months. I smiled at our VP and declared our plan would be christened the Better Than New Plan.

We got the top person at the bank on the phone and he could not believe our counteroffer. EVCOR's solution would actually look newer every year and since our machines were totally remanufactured they would probably work more efficiently for a longer period than our competitor's. EVCOR was presented the verbal order on the spot. We were ecstatic. Better Than New was born and went on to become one of EVCOR's all-time best revenue generators. The best thing about it was the profitability. We adjusted the plan and allowed an exchange every 18 months on a 36-month deal, which still permitted customers to achieve a three-for-one type of transaction. Quite a great deal and not precisely FREE but as close as it gets. The thought process is what you want to achieve.

Think big. Get big. If your firm markets any used or remanufactured items, this would be perfect for you.

Write it
down!

This a great example of counterpunching. Occasionally your competition will take actions you can't possibly see coming. Ask questions and be ready to leave the office and drive to the prospect's location to present a counteroffer. Don't give up—think up.

You versus Goliath

There is no "I" in team but there is in WIN.

Michael Jordan

If you had to choose between owning your largest competitor's corporate name or their entire customer base, which one would you pick?

I know experts talk about branding being very important but I would choose the entire customer base. Why? I could instruct my firm to improve the service response time and allow my sales force to upgrade the customer base. I could pinpoint all our efforts toward offering value-added solutions instead of looking for future customers.

With this in mind I proceeded to think of ways to acquire a behemoth's customer base at the lowest price possible.

I sat down in a quiet room with a pen and pad of paper, and these questions floated into view. What did my competitor sell? The answer was scales and mailing machines. What did

I want from them? Their customer base by model number would be nice.

GOT IT!! EVCOR would create a traditional mailer. It would have red ink printed on a white cardboard stock. This would appear commanding and substantial. Who would we address it to? Who is the portal providing access to America's larger firms? We decided to simply address it to the receptionist and printed a bold header on the front that screamed: THIS IS YOUR ANNUAL METER IMPRINT CLARITY TEST.

We requested specific steps be followed.

1. Please flip this card over.
2. Please update your address and phone number.
3. Set your postage meter to $00.00.
4. Run the card through the mail machine.
5. Place the metered mail card with the outgoing mail.
6. Thank you.

EVCOR sent this mailer to thousands of businesses—and waited.

WHOA! Within one week we were deluged with responses. I'm talking flooded.

It gets better! Our competitor leased five different models of postage meters to its customers. The imprints were all slightly different and included a unique serial number. EVCOR not only received the large corporation's customer base for the specific targeted ZIP codes but also could decipher the model numbers each client had. How did we know what model number they utilized? The indicia imprint is unique per model. It was a bonanza that allowed our sales force to infer which customers were large volume mailers versus small. We had a field day and immediately went after the largest firms.

Within a few months EVCOR suffered a counterattack. A bright yellow mailer was mailed into the specific ZIP codes we had attacked. Maybe it was yellow in color to symbolize "Yellow Journalism," which throughout the nineteenth century was promoted by Joseph Pulitzer and William Randolph Hearst. Yellow journalism represented sensationalistic reporting of the news and is partially blamed for United States starting the Spanish–American War.

Whatever. The mailer shouted EVCOR WAS PERPETRATING A SCHEME!! Man, was I mad—for about two minutes. Then I researched the word *scheme*. It is defined as "any systematic plan of action." You have to delve into the dictionary for a few minutes to find "a devious plan" but I believe the typical person thinks of something negative when they hear the word *scheme*. Now I was only mad the mail out did not state that EVCOR WAS PERPETRATING A DARNED GREAT SCHEME. It was brilliant. A little firm with minuscule resources had a huge, international competitor counterpunching after we had demonstrated we could take their customer base at will. Goliath was confused, angry, and blindsided. Cool.

We received a notice from our competitor's attorney announcing we could not use the word *annual* in our mailer since it was the first year EVCOR had mailed it. I promised to acquiesce and the skies cleared. What would our next move entail? Hmmm.

Write it
down!

Think about your industry. Can you send a mailer or an e-mail and capture your competitor's customer base? Why not? Do you sell office machines like copiers or computers? Try it. What if you sell software? Send the mailer to the receptionist and simply request the name of the current software product used by the firm.

The secret reason the mailer idea works is that no one else is attempting it. The request is unusual, providing the answer is harmless, and no formal company name is utilized. Do it, it works.

CHAPTER

38

Digitize Your Competition and Reposition

If I lose once it's a trend.

Pat Evans

You can train your mind to gain market share in your territory at the expense of your competitor. Draw a rectangle on a piece of paper—I'll wait. Okay? The boundaries of the rectangle represent a typical businessperson's internal parameters like, you can't use your competitor's name in ads. Even before a large competitor forces you back most companies try not to get the competitor's attorneys mad. By doing this they are cooperating with the competition. Now place a dot in the middle of the rectangle. This dot represents a harmless business like dry cleaners. EVCOR was designed to compete confidently using a guerrilla warfare approach. EVCOR created ad campaigns, which would shine light on a competitor's egregious actions. One competitor charged 32 percent simple interest buried in its lease. EVCOR exposed them in a mailer proclaiming this fact. EVCOR became much better known and increased our market share. We grew very fast and our

177

rectangle grew larger. We would expand the rectangle until we were literally pushed back. We would then create a new and different campaign starting with a larger rectangle than anyone else.

Now draw an arrow starting at the dot in the center and go up to the edge of the rectangle. This now represents where most competitors are located no matter what they sell. In the competitors' marketing minds and sales minds they have boxed themselves in. Remember this because it is very important. The competition has not pushed YOU back yet. Mentally you have just stopped competing at a certain imaginary level. It is somewhat like asking, "What does a fish in the ocean see when it looks up?" The correct answer is a mirror image of itself because it does not even know there is a sky up above the ceiling of water it inhabits.

The Competitive Rectangle is completed once you force yourself to push past the psychological boundaries inside your mind. Be BOLD! Design a plan of attack that emulates the arrow pushing past the boundaries of the rectangle. Keep being bold until your competitor pushes back with a legal warning or a unique plan of their own designed to stop you (see Figure 38.1). Your arrow is now well past the boundaries

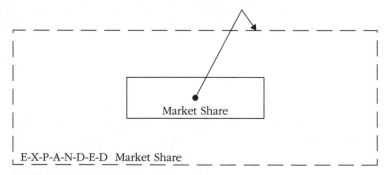

Figure 38.1 Competitive Rectangle

(even if you factor in pushback) and your market share has grown dramatically. Good for you.

As a sales rep or entrepreneur you need to "push the envelope." Study your competition. Go to a library or simply access the Internet. My first job after graduating from college was selling postage machines for Singer/Friden against the largest sellers of postage machines in the world. I found a history of one of my competitors in a Chicago library years ago. I also flew to San Francisco and read an entire lawsuit pertaining to one competitor versus an independent mailing equipment dealer. It was one of the largest/longest lawsuits in that district at the time.

I analyzed every bit of data I could get my hands on and then I "digitized" each competitor. One in particular was not a postage meter company. They were a leasing firm disguised as a mailing equipment company similar to McDonald's being a real estate company, not a fast food purveyor.

All other competitors before me had attacked with mail machines. My competitors had annihilated them. One of the largest firms in the United States was pushed out of the marketplace in 1951. They had simply attacked without analyzing the customer base. One of the entrenched competitors, a virtual monopoly, leased about 60 percent of its products, which means the typical customer was always on a long-term lease. The large competitor would have had to wait four years for the bulk of the customers to terminate their lease obligations. EVCOR introduced electronic shipping systems and competed against the competition's mechanical UPS meter placements. The EVCOR sales force knew to investigate any leases and to factor the additional costs into our quotations. I described the competitor's strengths and weaknesses on paper and asked the question, "How can the competitor be attacked by a much smaller entity, and is there a way to freeze the competitor so it cannot attack back?" You can lock yourself in a room and think about it with pen and paper ready and arrive at the sameμ answer I did.

EVCOR decided to expand the rectangle by attacking the competition's leasing base and utilizing the SalesBURST!! mentality. The competitor charged $51 per month for a mechanical meter that spit out UPS tapes with the shipping charges on them. The meter rental amount increased about 7 percent per year and the customer could never own it. EVCOR created the $49 Per Month Plan (so we would appear less from the get-go), and we increased the cost each year the same as the competitor's 7 percent. We allowed the customer to purchase the system at the end of 72 months (see Figure 38.2) for 10 percent

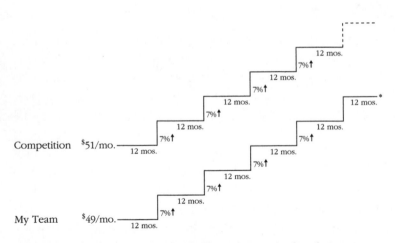

*Customer saves $2/mo. × 72 mos. = $144 saved. Customer has choice at 72 mos. (1) Purchase the system (exercise the buyout). (2) Continue to lease.

Figure 38.2 Step Lease

and offered more bells and whistles on the product. EVCOR changed the entire paradigm in the industry and our sales exploded exponentially. The Atlanta office alone increased from 9 systems per month to 19 per month. WOW! By the way, our system cost at least $2,500 less to a potential customer but we were having no luck selling them.

EVCOR leased tons of them with our new math-based leasing plan because we explained it to the customer in a different way. Why keep paying forever for an inferior technology that increased seven percent every year? More than one prospect informed us that when the math was reviewed our system was FREE. EVCOR was on its way to becoming an Inc. 500 winner and we had figured a way to "blow out the rectangle." EVCOR kept growing with our new plan until the competitor pushed back a few years later. Then we thought up a new angle.

Digitize your competition.

Have you read your competitor's literature, purchase agreements, lease agreements, and maintenance contracts? Have you visited and reviewed their entire web site? What do they do that is untrustworthy or illegal? Do they charge exorbitant leasing rates or extra high buyout amounts at the expiration of leases? Does the sales force quote services but the performance is less than anticipated? Come on, let's get competitive.

You assume, just like I did when I secured my first sales job out of college, that some other person in your firm has already done this. Number one, don't assume. Number two, you have better analytical skills than that other person. Do it yourself. You will feel more confident.

Good Luck and Good Selling!

Index

183

Special Offer!

Congratulations on purchasing *SalesBURST!!:* World's Fastest (entrepreneurial) Sales Training.

Here is the SPECIAL OFFER from the retailer:

- Purchase this book anywhere.
- Log on to salesburst.com.
- Enter in your name, e-mail address, where and the date the book was purchased.
- Click on the hyperlink to the retailer.
- Purchase a minimum of $175 worth of product (not including this book) from the retailer.

Receive a $20 discount immediately from the retailer. That's a savings of 11.4 percent!

Summary

- *SalesBURST!!* will show you how to make more money by closing deals faster.
- Buy the book and receive value from the retailer.
- Your book purchase helps fight Spina Bifida. Fifty-five percent of the net profits of the book are being donated to help alleviate medical expenses associated with Spina Bifida.
- You receive 11.4 percent savings from the retailer.

The offer expires three months after you purchase the book or no later than August 24, 2008. Patrick Evans, evanSales, Inc., John Wiley and Sons, Inc., salesburst.com, and the book seller are not redeeming the SPECIAL OFFER. You must retain your proof of purchase for the retailer. Thank you for purchasing *SalesBURST!!* The retailer retains the right to reject or cancel orders at its discretion.

Please visit salesburst.com as soon as possible and receive your $20 from the retailer.